Words of praise for Faith, Power, Joy

A deep perspective on family dynamics that inspires readers to better navigate their own lives. The author shares the stories and techniques of five generations of women who confront personal challenges and outmoded social norms with courage and determination as they grow spiritually and personally. Their transformation serves as a light, as they turn challenges into opportunities, deepen their faith, empower themselves, and share their joy! —Peter Kane, Counselor, Relationship Theorist and author of *The Monogamy Challenge: Creating and Keeping Intimacy*

A family of distinctive women share their secrets for overcoming adversity and transforming their lives. Heartfelt, inspiring and helpful!
—Dori H.

Faith, Power, Joy

Spiritual Guidance
From 5 Generations
of Remarkable Women

By

Sheryl A. Stradling

This is a work of fiction. Names, characters, places and incidents are either products of the author's imagination, or where factually based, are used fictitiously.

Book design by Sheryl A. Stradling

Cover design by Sheryl A. Stradling, Denise Cassino and Accurance

The author of this book does not dispense medical advice or prescribe the use of any technique as a form of treatment for physical, mental or medical problems without the advice of a physician, either directly or indirectly. The intent of the author is only to offer information of a general nature to help you in your quest for emotional and spiritual well-being. In the event you use any of the information in this book for yourself, which is your constitutional right, the author and publisher assume no responsibility for your actions.

Published by Dharma Press, LLC
Mesa, Arizona

Printed in the United States of America
First printing May 2017

ISBN 978-1-62747-037-7
E-Book ISBN 978-1-62747-040-7
ISBN numbers issued to Sojourn Publishing, LLC

Publisher's Cataloging-in-Publication
(Provided by Quality Books, Inc.)

Stradling, Sheryl A., author.
Faith, power, joy : spiritual guidance from 5 generations of remarkable women / by Sheryl A. Stradling.
pages cm
Includes bibliographical references.
LCCN 2017901532
ISBN 978-1-62747-037-7
ISBN 978-1-62747-040-7

1. Stradling, Sheryl A.--Family--Fiction. 2. Women--Psychology--Fiction. 3. Self-actualization (Psychology) --Fiction. 4. Spiritual formation--Fiction. 5. Life change events--Fiction. 6. Spirituality--Fiction. 7. Biographical fiction. I. Title.

PS3619.T7226F35 2017 813'.6
QBI17-900023

For more information, please visit the author's website
www.sherylstradling.com

Dedication

For my family, teachers and women everywhere.

May you find your faith, claim your power

and restore the world with your joy.

Let us, therefore, be willing to be measured;

not by what we have, but by what we give.

– A Search for God, Book I

Contents

Acknowledgments

Grateful acknowledgement is made to the following for permission to reprint copyrighted material, photos and original art.

The Christian Science Publishing Society. Permission to quote from the following:

(1) Peter B. Biggins, "Divine Love's Provision." *Christian Science Sentinel,* Vol. XXIX, No. 4, September 25, 1926.

(2) Bible Lesson Sermon, *Substance,* Sunday, September 12, 1926. *Science and Health with Key to the Scriptures,* Mary Baker Eddy, Section I (1) 335:12 and (2) 349:31.

(3) E. Violet J. Dicksee, "God Is All." *The Christian Science Journal,* Vol. 46, No. 3, June 1928.

The Polson Museum, Hoquiam, Washington. Photo of the Lytle Building, 1926, and photo of Ben K. Weatherwax drawing, "The Entrance," (originally published in the *Quinault,* Weatherwax High School yearbook, Vol. XVII, 1927).

The Seattle Times Company. "Wife Discards Husband's Name for Sake of Art; Court Sanctions Euphony Idea," *Seattle Sunday Times,* July 28, 1929, p. 7. Copyright © 1929.

University of Virginia, Department of Drama. "Play Surgery at Tryout Theatre," Minnie Moore McDowell, *Virginia Drama News,* Vol. XII, No. 8, 15 May 1944.

University of Washington Libraries, Special Collections. Images UW37868 (Wayfarer 1921 Principals in the Cast), and D. Kinsey A24 (Stand of Western Red Cedar Trees, Washington, 1913).

Whitworth University. Photo, Whitworth College Freshman Class 1914, and "Freshman Class History," by Minnie M. McDowell, *Whitworth College Bulletin,* 1914. Items located in the Whitworth University Archives, Spokane, WA.

Zeta Phi Eta. Minnie Moore McDowell, "Tryout Theatre." Material initially printed in *Cameo,* May 1944.

I'm grateful to everyone who helped me create this book.

Thank you, to all of my family, living and deceased. You have generated not only our DNA (totally randomly) but our history, traditions, spirit, inner strength and verve. You are all remarkable human beings. I especially thank my children; you are also my teachers and greatest joy.

Thanks also to all my incredible teachers in schools and colleges, special courses, weekend workshops, seminars, experiential and on-the-job training. Also thanks to the ministers in my churches, retreats and classes. You all inspired and encouraged me to grow, think, wonder, question and search. That's the greatest gift a teacher can give. You have contributed to my life's journey as well as to much of the knowledge and wisdom channeled into this book.

Writing a book is truly a shared effort. Many people have contributed in numerous ways. Thanks to my family – Starr, Geoff and Cecily – who unearthed memories, shared stories, and dug through boxes and heirlooms to find the photos, newspaper clippings and journals I needed. I couldn't have done the research without you. I also deeply appreciate my many friends and colleagues who encouraged me, listened to (and sometimes questioned) my ideas, and read and critiqued the manuscript. Special thanks to Dori, Joy, and others – you know who you are.

I'm grateful to Veola, my daughter, for sharing her devotionals, family stories, creative writing ideas and formatting expertise. Thanks to Bill, for accompanying me on three research trips, spending hours in libraries and museums, copying documents and writing pages of detailed notes. I'm also grateful to many others who over the years have been partners, close friends, lovers, mentors – and to others I've never met but whose books have opened new doors to wisdom.

A special thanks to John Larson, director of the Polson Museum in Hoquiam, Washington, for the "behind the scenes" tour and video on Ben K. Weatherwax; you brought him to life.

I am grateful also to many clerks and assistants in state, county and city offices and hospitals who searched for documents, and to librarians who helped in my research. Thanks to the librarians at the University of Washington (UW) Library Special Collections section, for helping me find what I needed and copying documents.

I also appreciate my genealogical society colleagues who did research for me and provided tips on breaking down my genealogy walls. I'm forever grateful to my professional work "tribe" of the last several years – the research scientists who inspired me with their own work, my supervisors, administrators and co-workers; you all helped me in your own perfect ways. And to all the people who read the manuscript, made recommendations and offered kind words – my heartfelt thanks. You are all awesome.

I was led to Tom Bird and his writing method by Kathy at my local herb shop. Thank you, and thanks to all in the Tom Bird program: Tom, Sabrina Fritts, Mary Stevenson, John Hodgkinson and the many experts who shared their knowledge. Denise Cassino, your practical expertise in everything about books has been wonderful. Thanks to the authors in my writing groups. You encouraged and inspired me as well as sharing your knowledge and experience.

And finally, I'd like to acknowledge and thank my spirit guides who continue to help me reveal the optimal path for my growth and highest good, and for nudging me in the right direction through rational thought, intuition, and abundant synchronicities. Spiritual guidance of the highest order led me along the trails and paths that inspired this book to come through me. I am grateful for this journey, as it has stirred me to expand my faith, embrace my power and share my joy.

Introduction

Family – We may not have it all together, but together we have it all.
– Unknown

Nothing happens by chance. We live in an ordered universe. Natural, immutable law prevails through absolute intelligence and consciousness. We call it God, Spirit, our Higher Power, First Principle, Reality, or Truth. Some feel no need to name it; it guides us nevertheless.

This energetic force which guides our lives, channels us along the pathways that bring us lessons and wisdom we need to learn through the exercise of our free will. We frequently follow circuitous paths to complete our learning. Often we repeat situations or put them aside until similar causes and conditions activate us again and we achieve what we are to know, understand and do.

It was no accident that I graduated from the Master Gardener program in the spring of 2010 after putting it on hold for fifteen years. I was exhilarated as I accepted my certificate. I knew this would usher in a new segment of my life. Of course it would make me a better gardener, but I felt in my heart that it was much more. Intuitively, I sensed I was starting on a journey that would lead me in directions I had no concept of at the time. My intuition was right.

In the Master Gardener program, trained volunteers assist the public with selecting, placing and maintaining healthy, climate-appropriate and environmentally responsible landscapes and gardens, based on scientific and area-specific research. The program is part of the land-grant university system nation-wide. After initial training and internship, a master gardener completes a required number of volunteer and education hours annually to maintain certification. Volunteer service involves educating the public about environmental and climate-appropriate plant selection and care, or supporting other program areas.

During my internship, I worked with a long-time master gardener who suggested that I write gardening articles for our on-line publication to obtain my required volunteer hours. Since I worked full-time, it was a great solution. I wrote my first article, "A Dirty Story," about reclaiming a damaged portion of my yard for a vegetable garden. It was published, and I continued writing, eventually completing five years of monthly gardening articles.

One evening while writing my article, I recalled that my mother, who'd also been a Master Gardener (in the first class of 1972-73), had written articles on gardening. I instantly recognized we had something in common that I'd never considered. We'd always been estranged. She had died thirteen years earlier and I regretted not knowing her better.

This realization preoccupied me. I wanted to know more. Why had she become a Master Gardener? What other commonalities did we share that I was unaware of? My curiosity led me to explore genealogy and family history, to interview family and friends, and travel on a research trip to the places my mother's family had lived. I discovered little personal information about her, so I expanded my search, including her mother and grandmother. My curiosity was piqued. I wondered what information I could discover about them that would relate to both me and my daughter.

As I learned more, I felt an overwhelming desire to share my knowledge. I first thought I might write only about my mother, but then felt an urge to share our family's chronicle. Delving into factual information and family myth led me to realize we all had more in common than I imagined. We were five generations of resilient, intriguing women. Courage and determination carried us through personal loss, financial challenges and grief as well as love, friendship and sharing. Although our times, circumstances and temperaments were different, we all learned lessons which led us to faith, power and joy.

This book, our story, is a work of "faction" – fiction based on fact. It recounts the saga of five generations of women in my maternal family line. I've included Mackie, my great-grandmother; Minnie, my grandmother; and Gail, my mother (all deceased), as well as myself and my daughter, Veola. I used historical facts as the background for the stories. Some details are yet to be found; others I chose not to use where they did not enhance the storyline or my artistic purposes. Where I had conflicting data or information I couldn't verify, I used what seemed intuitively right. Certain names and places have been changed for privacy; others are factual in order to celebrate them and their connection to our family.

I've always been a writer; it's a part of our family tradition. From my first primitive pencil-scrawled journals at twelve, which I hid in the unfinished portion of my bedroom closet, to the collaged and visual journals I create today, they have sustained my spirit and enhanced my life.

I write to understand myself and my world. My daughter is a Christian author of a series of books for middle grade children (*The Coin Chronicles*). My mother wrote short stories and articles, and my grandmother wrote articles about the theatre. Although I have no existing writing of my great grandmother's, I sense that she was led to write also. Perhaps I'll find hers yet.

My mother, Gail, wrote her life story in the 1970s. I quoted from it to enhance her story and used it as the basis for some of our conversations recorded in the book. I also used some of her letters and I'm grateful I saved as many as I did. I included a short story she wrote about her cats to illustrate her humorous and unique personality and share her love of her pets, because they were part of her support system. I edited it to fit the length and focus of this book.

My sister found our grandmother's journal and I incorporated some of her journal entries. I created a couple of entries that she might have written but were not in the time period of her journal (1930–1940). I also included entries from my own journals to illustrate my personal growth. My daughter contributed some of her devotionals and family stories to highlight her life.

My soul evolved through writing this book. Unearthing family stories enabled new questions, lost memories and unresolved feelings to surface. Incidents I thought I'd healed reappeared in new ways asking to be re-lived, experienced and understood differently. It was a new arena of personal and spiritual growth; one I couldn't rush through.

As I learned more about my ancestors and consequently myself, new healing emerged and understanding took the place of residual resentment or grief. Because of the research, writing and my personal growth, it took me six years to complete the book.

As I wrote, I often felt my ancestors' energies, feelings, and attitudes flow into my mind and heart. I felt three generations of women – Mackie, Minnie and Gail – hovering over me as I unearthed high school yearbooks, newspaper clippings, city directories, property records and photos. I felt them with me in spirit, encouraging me, guiding me, and providing intuitive hints as I pondered factual data and family lore.

I often spontaneously received an inward sense of where to look for information, why a decision was made or how they felt when a spouse died or they faced a financial crisis. I realized that many of their trials and responses to life's challenges were similar to my own. I verified the facts I could and considered the remainder intuitive guidance.

The more I delved into each woman's life, the more passionate I felt about sharing our inspirational stories. The more I was moved by our demonstrations of faith, energized by our power as women, and exhilarated by our joy, the stronger I felt about sharing it now. I couldn't wait until I verified every fact.

My resolve also grew because I felt I might run out of time. I had missed interviewing my mother and her siblings, since they are deceased. During my research, I interviewed two elderly women, long-time family friends; they both passed shortly afterwards. I interviewed my deceased uncle's wife, who was also elderly, and concerned about her failing memory. I was fortunate to talk with her when I did, as her memories continue to fade.

I firmly believe we come into our lives to learn specific lessons and develop in unique ways that our souls require for their ultimate growth. I believe that we as family carry not just our DNA and the results of our nature and nurture, but spiritual commonalities and a collective family consciousness that carries through generations. We are related in spirit and energy as well as physically, mentally and emotionally.

Family truly is forever. The influence of family on our lives is immense. What we do with it is another matter. In my family of origin, my first role was to question and rebel, the next was to investigate and understand, and my final is to celebrate. How's that for a complete turnaround?

If we can accept, celebrate and judge – but not condemn – ourselves and our families, we can become better people, be closer to our loved ones, enjoy happier lives, and deepen our personal and spiritual natures.

I hope this book will inspire you to take another look at your own family – an open-minded look, a far-reaching look – and be able to understand with compassion, forgive where forgiveness is needed, love unconditionally, and celebrate *your* family's unique and perfect contribution to our human family.

With Peace, Love and Light,

Sheryl A. Stradling
May 2017

Primary Characters

Lest we forget – from Joyce's journal, 1936

Family Members, deceased

Charlotte Moore McDowell Shock (Lottie or Mackie) 1874–1934
My great grandmother; Minnie's mother; Gail, Joyce & Jud's grandmother

Thomas J. McDowell (T. J. or Tom) 1859–1908
My great grandfather – Mackie's first husband; Minnie's father

Joseph Alexander Shock (Schock; Daddy Joe) 1883–1926
Mackie's third husband

James Benton (J. B.) Kesterson (Ben, Uncle Ben or Mr. Kay) 1859–1954
Mackie's second and fourth husband

Minnie Moore McDowell Klingberg (McDowell, MMM or Minnie Moore McDowell) 1894–1949
My grandmother; Gail, Joyce and Jud's mother

Karl John Klingberg (KJK or Kling) 1879–1953
My grandfather; Minnie's husband (later divorced)

Judson T. Klingberg (Jud, born Donn) 1916–1986
My uncle; Gail and Joyce's brother

Joyce Klingberg Guberlet (Trudi) 1920–2006
My aunt; Gail and Jud's sister

Gail C. Klingberg Stradling 1918–1998
My mother

Richard H. Stradling, Jr. (Dick) 1917–1991
My father

Stephanie G. Stradling 11/1951–12/1951
My sister, Dick and Gail's daughter

Stand of Western Red Cedar Trees, Washington, 1913. University of Washington Libraries, Special Collections, D. Kinsey A24. Notice the man standing next to the tree on the far left.

1 ~ Trust Yourself

Your heart will always tell you what's working and what's not.
– Sarah Ban Breathnach

1890 – Olympic Peninsula, Chehalis (Grays Harbor) County, Washington

What will the lucky marbles win?

I let my intuition guide me.

Fine crystalline mist settled over the dense cedar treetops one hundred fifty feet above ground. The sky grayed deeper as the sun dropped lower on the horizon. Below, tangled underbrush competed with salmonberry, vine maple and oxalis for the diminishing daylight. Mosses, spike ferns and lichens festooned the ancient tree trunks. Across the meadow, a rustic farmhouse raised its roof into the mist. Smoke slowly swirled upward from the chimney. Inside, the aroma of freshly baked bread, roasted vegetables and chicken stew spread the welcoming atmosphere of dinner. A crackling fire's smoky odor filled the main room.

Ellen heard talking and laughing emerging from the back porch. She wiped her hands on her stained cotton apron and turned toward the stove. She lifted the cast iron lid off the huge pot of stew. The rich scent of tender chicken, chunks of carrots, celery and white beans assailed her nostrils. She stirred it briefly, and reached in with her sampling spoon. She lifted out a spoonful of chicken, broth and beans, held it in front of her lips and blew on it to cool it. She tilted her head, sipped the broth and then tasted the chicken and beans.

"Ummm. This is mouth-watering, tender and spicy. That pepper did the trick. It needs a little salt though," she murmured. She grabbed a large pinch of salt, threw it in, and stirred it again. She replaced the heavy lid and moved the pot to the back of the old iron stove.

"We're home," Samuel called, as he stuck his head around the corner. He pulled off his faded jacket. "I guess you saw us coming up the path. I brought some people for dinner tonight. T. J., Ben Kesterson and "Joe" Johansen are with me. John and Mary are right behind us."

Everyone crowded into the back porch, taking off damp jackets and hanging them on the row of wooden pegs. Mary took off her heavy wool coat and hung it, straightening it so it wouldn't wrinkle.

T. J. reached into his pocket and pulled out a handful of marbles as he pulled his damp jacket off and hung it on the last peg. He quickly shoved them into his pants pockets and pulled his shirt down before walking into the house.

"Still got your marbles, T. J.?" Ben asked as he followed him in. He slapped T. J. on the back and smirked. "Just checking!"

T. J. laughed. His gray eyes sparkled. He rubbed his chin. "You know me," he replied with a grin. He stuck his hand in his pocket again. The clink of marbles sounded softly under his clothing.

"We're serving now," Ellen called from the main room. "Come in and make yourselves at home." She motioned to Lottie, sixteen, and Emma, fourteen. "You girls can help me serve. Lottie, watch Effie and Ernest too – keep them out of the way while we serve."

"All right, Momma," Lottie replied. She got up from the table. She was slender; tall for her age, almost six feet. She quickly pulled back her dark curls, tied her white ruffled apron around her waist and straightened her long flour-sack skirt. She bent over and grabbed Effie, a toddler, sitting among a pile of wooden blocks on the floor, and stuck her fingers under her cottony shirt. "Watch out, I'm going to tickle you." Effie squealed. Lottie slung her on her hip, holding her with one arm while she gathered up the well-used silverware from the counter with the other hand.

"Hold on to me, Effie, while we set the table. Come here, Ernest. You sit right here." She pointed to his high chair. "I'll help you up in a minute. It's dinner time." She set the places quickly, and put Effie in her chair. She lifted Ernest into his high chair and pushed it up to the table.

So many chores all day long. I know there's something better just waiting for me. She sighed, turned to the stove, took the hot bread from the oven, and set the loaves on the rough-hewn cutting board with a knife and a dish of freshly churned butter.

Ellen set well-used linen napkins at the places. She paused and looked around the room, taking a mental inventory. "We'll serve at the table tonight, girls." She turned toward Frank, who was the same age as Emma. "Make sure we have all the chairs. Bring in that wooden bench from the porch too."

The men came in and stood by the table talking. Mary followed them. "Can I help you, Ellen?" she asked.

Ellen shook her head. "Everything's ready." She gestured toward the table. "Everyone, please sit down." The seats filled quickly. Emma put the plates and bowls on the table. Lottie set white ceramic tureens of steaming stew in the center with ladles. The hearty aroma wafted through the room. Ellen served the platters of baked potatoes, carrots and squash. Lottie brought the three loaves of freshly baked bread and the butter, and set them at the end of the table. She took off her apron and hung it over her chair as she sat down between the younger children.

"This smells scrumptious, Ellen," Mary said. "Thanks for having us over. I'll return the favor next week."

Samuel pulled out his chair and sat at the head of the table. "Everyone is welcome here tonight. Let's pray." He bowed his head and folded his rough hands. Stillness filled the room as the fire crackled and everyone settled into their chairs. "Thank you, dear Lord, for another safe day in the woods. Bless this meal and all who are here. Amen."

Ellen served the stew while others passed food around the table. Silence ensued as everyone eagerly filled their plates. The fire hissed and crackled softly, accenting the quiet clink of silverware against the dishes. The platters of food emptied quickly.

"What a great meal, Ellen," Ben said. "Thanks. I sure was hungry after a week of working in the woods. I was short of rations last week. I lived on rice and beans for a day." He laughed. "I made up for it tonight though."

The others nodded and joined in. "Yes, it was hearty. It hit the spot. We were all hungry after a day's work." They pushed their chairs back, ready to relax in the warmth of the fire.

Samuel grabbed a couple of bottles of applejack and glassware from the cupboard and set them on the table. "This'll warm you all up. Help yourselves while I go out back and bring in more wood for the fire." He turned and walked out through the porch to the shed.

"I'll pour," Ben said, standing up as he as he opened the bottles. His tall rangy frame cast a long shadow on the wall. The light flickered over his blonde hair. He picked up a bottle, lifted it cautiously to his nose and sniffed it. "It smells mighty strong. That'll make for a good time tonight." He laughed and looked around the room. "I don't know about you guys, but I've been drinking nothing but water for a week. I just got in tonight, haven't even been home yet. I can tell you that timber up north is going to be worth a lot; the trees are big and dense. It's mostly cedar, too. I cruised the whole stand; it was a lot of walking over steep terrain. I counted and measured all the trees. My client will be happy with the money he'll get for it."

"Sounds like more work for us," John said.

"Yeah," Joe added. "Somebody's crews will have to log it. You could go in with us, Ben. You used to be a logger. You were a farmer before that. Why did you turn to timber cruising?

Ben poured a shot in his glass and took a sip. He looked at John and Joe thoughtfully. "I can support my family now. Cruising is an independent job. I usually work alone or with a partner. We trek through the wilderness into virgin forest to locate timber claims for people. I love the woods, know my way around. Nothing compares to finding that 'biggest tree' and I can usually scale or estimate the amount of timber in it very close to the cut amount. It's satisfying and I get paid well."

"Well, I don't blame you, but I think I'll stick to logging," Joe replied.

John nodded in agreement. "We usually don't work all year, but it's the trade I know."

Ben passed glasses of applejack around. He handed one to T. J. *He's a peculiar guy. Never talks about himself and always has those marbles. He makes everyone laugh, though. He's no stranger to hard work; he's got the build of a bear and he can hold his own with the best of the loggers or laborers. Got to admire him for that.*

Lottie cleared the table, quickly sweeping up the plates and stacking them, piling the silverware on top and setting them in the large apron sink. Ellen lit the lanterns as the room turned darker from the fading light. Shadows flickered across the wall from the fire in the stone fireplace. "Come on Ernest, Effie and Frank. It's time for bed." Ellen picked up Effie and escorted the other children to their shared room in the back of the cabin. She turned back and called, "Emma, you finish up the dishes now, and then come help me get the little ones to bed."

John took his glass of applejack and moved his chair closer to the fire. He sat down and took a sip. "Oh, this is mighty good. It's savory like fresh green apples, spices and sweet caramel. A perfect end to a great meal." He set his glass at the end of the table. "Hey, T. J., do you have any of those marbles in your pockets?" He gave T. J. a grin. "I might want to bet you tonight."

"You know I always have marbles in my pockets – the lucky ones. And I can beat you at any bet you want to make." T. J. took a drink. He set his glass down, walked over to the fire and stood with his back to it, his feet shoulder width apart. His stretched and put his hands on his hips. His stocky build seemed larger as the light from the fire played around his figure. He cocked his head and looked at John. "Well?"

"Well, you sure enough proved that last week," John said. He leaned forward and shook his fist at him in a mocking gesture. "Land sakes! I lost half my lunch to you. I was thinkin' I might win that back."

T. J. grinned. "I wouldn't count on it. Your lunch was mighty good, too." He put on a show of licking his lips. "Roast beef. I don't get that very often." He put his hand in his pocket. The soft click of ceramic marbles rubbing against each other filled the quiet room.

Mary looked at T. J. quizzically. "Why do you carry marbles in your pockets?"

He smiled. "Luck. When I need to decide something important, I pull one out and see if my hunch is right. If it's the right color, I go ahead. I collect 'em too, but only the lucky ones."

"How do you know which ones are lucky?" Mary asked.

T. J. turned from the fire and looked at her. "Oh, I just feel it. My lucky marbles helped me decide to come west. My buddy back home gave them to me. After the Civil War, our family split up. Most were Union, but not all. We West Virginians are pretty independent, you know. As time went on, the disagreements got worse; brothers and cousins were opposed; couldn't forgive each other. Times were hard as we tried to rebuild our farms. My dad was disabled in the war, too. My marbles helped me make the decision to move on. I had a hunch that if I picked the right marble, it would bring me good luck. It did. I came out West and never looked back."

He glanced around the room. "Do I have any takers?" T. J. looked at Ben and grinned. "I know it won't be you, Ben; you've got too many kids to feed." He laughed and looked around again. "Hey, Lottie, how about you?" He motioned to her. "You wanna bet me?" He grinned and looked at her with a raised eyebrow. He rubbed his hands together. "I'm feeling lucky tonight."

"Well . . ." she hesitated. "Oh, T. J., you're such a tease!" She laughed, and her dark eyes sparkled. She tilted her head and leaned forward as she studied him. "I think I *will* bet you tonight. Why not? I dare you to pull out three of the blue mottled ones; they're the Benningtons, right?" She looked at him expectantly.

He nodded. "Yep, they're the blue ones. Only the fancy ones have other colors." He stepped closer to her.

She flashed him her biggest smile. "If you can do it, I'll make you a pie next week when you come for dinner. If you lose, you'll have to do what I say."

"Oh, this is getting good." Ben stood up, turned his chair around, pulled it closer to the group and sat down backwards on it, leaning forward against the chair back. He thrust his long arms out and motioned to her. "Yeah, Lottie, don't worry, he's not that lucky. He's plumb crazy. I don't know how he beat me before I took off for the woods. For sure his luck can't hold. He'll be workin' for you all next week. You can give him women's chores see how he does with 'em."

John spoke up. "I beat him about a month ago. He couldn't hornswoggle me. He had to work extra to help me that day. He wasn't happy about it either." He raised his glass of applejack as if to make a toast and took a swig. "Here's to whippin' T. J. again." He grinned. "It's all in fun of course. My fun and his work. I like it that way."

Joe laughed. "This is the best bet I've heard yet. Good luck, Lottie."

Lottie glanced around the group. She felt tingly all over. This was exciting. She'd never thought about betting with him before, but why not? She was adventurous. Usually it was just the men who bet him. Whoever lost had to trade workloads, help each other at the end of the day or share their meals to pay up. She looked at T. J. curiously. *I wonder how he can pick the right marbles. I'm sure it's just luck. I'm as lucky as he is. Probably luckier.*

T. J. gazed at her intently. His hand was in his pocket. A hint of a smile crossed his face. He laughed softly. The marbles clinked against each other again. He shifted position, walked around the group and returned, stopping closer to her. He studied her intently.

Mary glanced at Lottie and caught her eye. "Lottie, he's just joking. He doesn't have that many marbles. I've seen him pull them out before. We all know you're luckier than he is. We women are intuitive – we have more grit, too." She winked at Lottie and lowered her voice. "They're just marbles. How would he know?"

Lottie leaned over and whispered, "He just *thinks* he can win." Mary smiled and nodded.

T. J. looked at Lottie again. "Okay, Miss Lottie, I'm ready when you are."

Lottie studied him. Her dark eyes flashed as she looked at T. J. and then at Mary. She arranged her long skirt and sat up straighter. "Okay, I'm ready. You'll be in for a lot of trouble if you lose, T. J. It'll take you a long time to work this off, you know."

She pictured the marbles in his pocket. The Benningtons were special. They were pretty glazed clay, mottled light and dark blue with "eyes" on them; spots that were lighter where the marbles had touched each other when fired. Blue was her favorite color and three felt like a lucky number. She smiled to herself.

She studied T. J. closely. He was a jokester, always making people laugh. She wondered if he was serious now. It would be easy to bake him a pie if he won. But if he lost? What then? A special feeling rose suddenly in her heart. She felt drawn to him as if they shared something special. She sensed that her challenge was more than just a dare. She studied him as he stood by the table, watching her in return.

Even at sixteen, she sensed that something extraordinary was ahead for her – not just having babies and living on the farm like her parents. She called it her "sixth sense." A shiver quickly ran through her body. She trembled slightly. She unclasped her hands and pushed her dark hair back. She wondered what the chances were of him really having the three blue marbles and being able to pick them from his pocket sight unseen.

He probably didn't have a chance. She felt a flutter in her heart. Would she have to decide his fate – and hers too?

"What's he's gonna owe you when he loses, Lottie?" Ben asked. He got up and moved his chair closer. He sat backwards on it again, leaning forward with his arms folded on the back of it, his legs stretched out. He looked at her and grinned.

Lottie smiled slightly. She glanced at T. J. Her eyes were on fire now. She sensed her power. She looked him up and down. This was the biggest bet anyone had ever made with him. All the other times, it was just in fun, a way to pass the time and laugh. She felt butterflies in her stomach. She looked around the group again. She glanced at Mary for encouragement. Mary smiled. She pulled her worn red shawl around her shoulders, leaned toward T. J. and focused her gaze on him.

She cleared her throat. "We'll see," she said quietly. "Okay, T. J., I'm ready. Let's see what you have there."

"Yeah," John called out. He stood up, his short, wiry frame a contrast to T. J.'s tall, husky one. He picked up the applejack and poured himself another shot. "You've had it now, T. J. You're gonna be in a fix if you lose."

T. J. stepped forward. He grinned. He rolled up the sleeves of his faded blue flannel shirt and rubbed his hands together. "I'll take you up on that," he said, laughing. His face and sandy hair caught a glint of light from the fire. He straightened his shoulders and wiped his hands on his pants.

"I have two pockets. I get two tries. Agree?"

Lottie nodded silently.

He put his right hand in his pocket, turning the marbles over and over. The soft clink of the hand-fired clay marbles filled the air as everyone grew silent. His gaze shifted. He stared into the fire as it crackled and hissed softly. He concentrated on the feel of the marbles in his pocket.

The quiet clink of marbles seemed to stretch time. T. J. felt the cold round orbs in his pockets. He was sure he had what he needed. But could he pick the right ones by feel? Hand-made marbles weren't all perfectly round. And the salt glaze on each one had a special feel. Benningtons had a slightly rough, pitted surface. Although polished, they had a dull finish, soft to the touch. The polished marbles were smoother with less pitting.

Slowly he pulled his right hand out of his pocket, fist closed, and held it out. "This is just the beginning," he declared.

He opened his hand. In it were two beautiful blue polished Benningtons, mottled with dark and light blue spots. They caught the light of the fire. A slightly smaller brown marble was next to them. He held his hand out to show Lottie.

She gasped. The group murmured in response.

"I have one more chance. You agreed, right?"

She looked at him, nodding slowly. Silence filled the room again as everyone leaned forward to watch.

He shoved his left hand into his pocket. Once again, the clink of marbles softly accompanied the fire's sizzling. T. J. felt the marbles as he carefully rolled them between his fingers. He studied Lottie's face. She stared at him wide-eyed. She looked excited. Her dark eyes glowed.

He shifted position, tilted his head and studied her again. *I wonder what she'd do if she won. She's mighty pretty. She's nice too, and she has nerve.* He chuckled quietly to himself. He closed his fingers around the marbles in his pocket.

"Let's see . . ."

Slowly he pulled his hand out, fist closed. He opened it and held his hand out to her. In it rested one polished black marble and two fancy Benningtons mottled with brown, blue and a hint of green.

He looked straight into her eyes. She caught her breath. He'd lost the bet. Now she had to make her decision.

The room instantly became an uproar of noisy talking and shouting. "She did it – she beat him. Congratulations! We knew a woman could win against him."

Mary exclaimed, "Tell him he has to marry you, Lottie. He'll have to work for you forever then."

"Yeah," John said. "I dare you. Tell him that. That'll fix his wagon for good."

Joe let out a large guffaw. "Well, I declare."

Ben clapped. "I knew he'd lose this one. Make it good, Lottie. We're counting on you."

Her eyes sparkled. She smiled broadly as she looked at T. J. She felt her heart flutter again. Her lips parted. An intuitive thought flashed through her mind. *It's him. He's the one. He's so easy to get along with – light hearted, funny – smart – he's like family. Why not?* Her pulse raced. She felt her heart fill with emotion. Color crept into her cheeks. She eyed him intently as her mind sped from one thought to another. *This is my destiny. It's been right here in front of me all along. Oh dear God, I feel this is so right; I've been brought to this moment by God's grace. I always knew something special was waiting for me. This is my time. I feel it in my heart. I know my decision.*

"How about it, T. J.?" she said, scrutinizing him. "You lost the bet. Now you have to do as I say." She paused, looking down momentarily. Then she looked up, deep into his eyes. "I think we should get married," she said softly.

Ben jumped up from his chair, almost knocking it over. "Hey T. J., you're gonna be a married man at last. We'd about given up on you!"

T. J. took two steps forward and stood in front of her. *I hadn't thought about marriage before, but this just feels right.* He reached out, gently took her hand, opened it, and put the marbles in it. "I told you they were lucky. Even though I lost the bet, I won you. I guess I'd better ask your father now and make it official." He laughed, the laugh lines around his eyes making him handsome. He looked into her eyes. "I'm so happy," he whispered. "Will you really marry me?"

Lottie McDowell, c. 1894

She grasped the marbles tightly in her hand and looked at him. Tears formed in the corners of her eyes. "Yes, I'd love to."

His eyes sparkled as he looked into hers and smiled. "You know I always know which marbles are lucky. That's why I carry 'em."

She wiped her wet cheeks with the back of her hand, smiled and gazed into his eyes. "I know," she said softly.

She felt her heart expand as if it could encompass the entire universe. *My sixth sense was right. It was meant to be. I am blessed.* She felt God smiling on them. She felt her faith expand. "I know this is right," she whispered to herself as much as to him.

They were married in a simple ceremony at her parent's home on May 18, 1890. She was sixteen, he was thirty-one. They settled nearby in Ocosta, where T. J. had repaired an abandoned woodsman's cabin.

Minnie, their only child, was born in 1895. T. J. worked in a variety of jobs in the area. He worked in the mills, as an auto mechanic and as a mechanic for the railroad. A true entrepreneur, he bought and sold property, opened two furniture stores in Montesano, later sold them and opened a hardware store where he did very well. They moved to south Tacoma in late 1906 or early 1907 so he could pursue new job opportunities in the furniture business.

1902–1906 – Montesano, Washington

Minnie –a precocious child

I am a jewel buried deep in stone.

Lottie bustled around the warm, cozy kitchen. The aroma of braised veal roast with vegetables and gravy, cornbread and peach cobbler filled the house. Minnie, around eight or nine years old, perched on a wooden chair next to the kitchen table. She banged her feet repeatedly against the chair legs and spindle. Her chin rested on her chest as she stared at the floor, scowling.

"Oh, Mother, do I have to?"

"Now, McDowell, you know what I told you. You're having your photo taken at three o'clock. It's time to get ready. Your dress looks so pretty. Sit still! I have to curl your hair. I want to put these pretty white ribbons in it."

"Why? I want to ride my bike now. My friends are waiting for me outside. I told them to wait. They always do what I say. I want to go outside *now*. I don't like this dress. It's too stiff." She squirmed in the chair, tossing her head.

"Hold still. I'm curling your hair. I want your long ringlets to show in this photo. They will be so lovely with the bows in them. Your dress is beautiful. You want to look pretty, don't you?"

"No. I don't care. I want to play now." She grimaced and stood up abruptly, putting her hands on her hips. "I don't need my hair curled. I don't want ribbons. I want to ride my bike."

"Oh, McDowell, you're just like your father. You know that's why I call you by his name. You're so dramatic and stubborn. You can't have your way with everything. Your friends can wait. I told you before that you were going to have your picture taken today. The photographer will be here in ten minutes. Now sit down. I'm almost done."

"I am, Mother." She slumped into the chair and stared at the wooden floor.

"You'll be able to ride your bike and play in a few minutes. Remember to sit still again while he takes the picture. When he's done you can change your clothes."

"All right, Mother. She pouted. "I remember. You told me that already."

Lottie's thoughts focused on Minnie as she fluffed the sleeves of her dress and arranged her long, dark curls. *I love her so. But she's so old for her age and different from other children. She has a mind of her own. She's very determined. She asks so many questions and she won't accept any answer except the one she wants to hear. She's just like her father. I don't know what I'd do if I had another like her.*

Minnie Moore McDowell
c. 1904, around ten years old

2 ~ Flexibility Enables Change

Don't be afraid to cry. It will free your mind of sorrowful thoughts.
– Hopi

1908–1909 – Tacoma, Washington

T. J.'s health challenge

Often the test of courage is not to die but to live. – Orestes

T.J. waited patiently in the doctor's office. He shifted his position in the hard chair, bending forward so his back wouldn't press against it so painfully. The swelling and fatigue had forced him to come today. He recalled what the doctor had told him – it was his kidneys. He'd experienced a fever, nausea and unusual swelling of his legs and ankles the night before. He'd been sick off and on for about a year. At times, he was too sick to work, but lately he was better – until last night.

Dr. Anderson opened his office door. "Mr. McDowell, please come in. How are you feeling?"

"I had some bouts of pain last night, blood in my urine, and more swelling than usual. I think I passed a kidney stone. That's why I'm here."

"You probably did. Bright's disease [acute or chronic nephritis] is a serious kidney disease. You've done surprisingly well in the last year. Unfortunately, it's probably gotten worse. We'll check your blood pressure today. Your face is swollen again. That's a sign of edema or fluid retention. There is no successful treatment for chronic Bright's disease at this time. The standard treatment includes local depletion or bloodletting to decrease blood pressure, hot baths, bed rest, diuretics and laxatives. We've talked about that before."

"Doctor, I can't do that. I have to work every day. I have a store to run. My customers depend on me. I'm busy unloading new shipments, helping my customers with deliveries and moving heavy furniture. I can't be weak. I need my strength." He paused, eyeing the doctor. "I don't want my wife to know that it's gotten worse. She'll just worry. You understand, don't you, Dr. Anderson?"

"This is a serious disease, Mr. McDowell. I can't stress that enough. You need to take care of yourself."

"I think I can manage. I feel pretty good most of the time. I can rest in the evenings. When I have too much pain, I just close the store or have my wife tend it."

"You need to come back and see me if your symptoms get worse. I want to make sure you're all right."

T. J. left the doctor's office frowning. *I have to hide this from Lottie. She'll just worry. There's nothing she can do. The doctor didn't even know what to do. I can't believe he thought I'd let him take my blood and then stay in bed. How am I supposed to work? I have to be active. It makes me feel better. I can lick this. I just need time.*

Lottie later recalled what happened after he finally told her what the doctor had said:

He'd had symptoms for about a year, but they were mostly mild. He stayed home from work for a while and got somewhat better. He was the type of man who never complained. He had a positive attitude about everything. He worked hard and enjoyed life. I don't think I ever would have known how serious it was if he hadn't kept going to the doctor.

One night after dinner, his pain came on stronger than usual. He got into bed and elevated his legs. The swelling had always gone down before, but that night was different. He was retaining fluid, and he was swollen all over, especially in his lower body. I bathed him with cold damp rags to keep his temperature down. We didn't know what else to do. I was so worried, but he seemed to take it in stride. We had relatives nearby, Mae and John Cook, so I sent Minnie to their house a few blocks away to spend the night and tell them we needed the doctor – but he never came. Late that night, T. J. felt better and slept some.

He woke up around 2:00 AM, feverish and swollen. He'd gotten much worse. He said he felt like he was drowning in his own body fluids. His skin was so tight he thought he would burst. I felt so helpless. He told me to go over to the Cooks, wake them and get help. I didn't want to leave him, but he insisted.

The winter rain pounded on the windows and the wind whipped the trees back and forth. I put on my heavy coat and half-walked, half-ran through the rain to their house and woke them up. They hurriedly got dressed and came back with me, but it was too late. He lay in the bed as if he was sleeping, but his heart had stopped. The excess fluids had killed him. He died of dropsy [edema] that night.

I sat by his bed in shock. His skin, once so ruddy, was now pale. I took his hand in mine and held it tenderly. I whispered softly, "I'll always love you." I felt so guilty about leaving him there alone, even though I had to get help. I bowed my head, started to cry and couldn't stop. Mae tried to console me, but I was inconsolable. I couldn't think of anything, except that he was gone and it was partly my fault.

The next day I bought a family plot at the Tacoma Cemetery nearby. He was buried the day after. That night after Minnie went to bed, I was alone for the first time. I'd never really been alone. I went from my family right into marriage. I sat at the kitchen table, my head in my hands. I sank into the chair as grief swept through me. A wave of fear suddenly overcame me. What was I going to do now? Then sadness overwhelmed me and I started crying again. I bowed my head and prayed silently. *Dear Father, I've lost him. He's gone to You now. Keep him safe in Your arms. Help him know that he's free. His suffering is over.*

A sob caught in my throat. I continued to pray. *Oh Lord, please help me. I'm alone now. Help our family. I don't know what to do. Please help Minnie; she's so young.* I sat mutely, eyes closed, trying to find the right words. Then I felt a gentle, loving energy envelop me. Peace settled on me like a warm, protective blanket. I sensed T. J.'s presence around me, comforting me. I was so grateful. *Thank you, Lord, for bringing me peace now. I know he is at peace too. I pray for your guidance. Please give me the strength to care for Minnie and do what I must.*

T. J. died on December 7, 1908. His death at forty-nine transformed our lives. I was thirty-three when he died; Minnie was thirteen. I cried for days from the shock, and from my guilt at leaving him alone to die. I relied on Mae and friends to help me make decisions. I was grateful that T. J. had belonged to the Ancient Order of United Workmen, Knights of the Maccabees and Woodmen of the World. As fraternal benefit societies, they provided insurance for death benefits. The Woodmen also provided a beautiful marker for his grave. He'd planned ahead for us.

I took over his furniture business. I'd helped him with it when we lived in Montesano. I notified his customers about his illness and death. When I explained to them who I was and what happened, they started calling me "Mackie" and the nickname stuck. Many stopped by the house to bring food. Others helped me sort out the unsold furniture and reorganize the store. Some bought additional items just to help me. I sold the remaining furniture to another business and closed the store.

I wanted to go back to Montesano to be near family and friends, so we moved in early 1909. I rented the entire upper floor of the Byles building and took in boarders. I was happy to be back and I planned to stay there, but our lives changed again.

1909–1915 – Montesano and Tacoma, Washington

Mackie transitions to a new life.

Every moment is open to change.

Mackie and Minnie settled into their new living quarters in Montesano. Mackie was busy with her boarders, cooking and cleaning. She heard a knock at the door. "Just a minute." She walked to the door and pulled it open.

"J. B. Kesterson! What a nice surprise. We haven't seen each other in a few months, Ben. You must have been tramping through the woods a lot." She laughed.

"I have been. I'm still a timber cruiser, and I travel all over Chehalis County, estimating the amount of timber in a stand. They call me Uncle Ben now because I've been around so long." He smiled.

"Well, my nickname has changed too; it's Mackie now. It started when I closed T. J.'s store, but local Montesano folks still call me Lottie." She gestured to the front room. "Please come in. It's good to see you." She gave him a hug. He put his arm around her affectionately. His round, wire-rim glasses sat slightly crooked on his nose. His neatly trimmed moustache and hair were speckled with gray now.

"Please sit down. I'll get us some tea and pie and we can talk." She stepped into the small kitchen, poured two cups of tea, cut slices of pie and put the dishes on a silver tray. She brought it to the living room, set it on the table and sat down.

Ben smiled at her. "Thank you. This is a real treat. Apple pie is my favorite." He took a bite. "Delicious. You're a good cook like your mother." He put down the fork and focused his eyes on her intently. "It's good to see you, Lottie. We haven't seen each other since our touring-car trip to Seattle in June. I really enjoyed that. I'm taking a break from work for a while. I'd love to spend some time together like we talked about on the trip."

Mackie's eyes sparkled. "I'd enjoy that very much. I've been so busy with my boarders that I haven't taken time to do anything else. It's a bigger commitment than I thought. Someone always seems to need something. I'll ask my sister if she could take over for a week or two. I'm sure she wouldn't mind. We could take another trip or just relax."

He reached over and took her hand. "That would be wonderful." He leaned closer to her and looked into her eyes. "I'm serious, Lottie. We're both alone now. We've known each other a long time. I thought about this all the months I was working in the woods. Let's spend some time together and see how things work out."

Mackie squeezed his hand in return. She felt an internal rush of energy and the familiar flutter in her heart. She beamed at him. "Nothing could make me happier. I've been lonely too. It's been almost a year since T. J. died." She sighed softly. "I'm ready to move on with my life now."

J. B. Kesterson, c. 1930

Ben and Mackie were married on November 9, 1909. He was fifty – the same age that T. J. would have been. She was thirty-five. She moved back to south Tacoma near the house where she and T. J. had lived. With Ben's help, she started another boarding house. He maintained his residence in Montesano and continued to work in the area. He stayed with her when he came to town. She moved to Seattle a few years later, where she also ran a boarding house for local workingmen. She and Ben (whom my family always called "Mr. Kay") stayed together for a few years and then divorced, probably because of their differing lifestyles and ages.

Minnie stayed with Mr. Kay for the summer of 1910. She helped him with his business and housekeeping while her mother got settled and set up the boarding house. She later stayed with the Cooks, their relatives, in south Tacoma. She and their daughter, Etha, were the same age.

Minnie never talked about losing her father. She learned from their tragedy that education was her key to independence and security. She loved learning and excelled in school. She was a natural leader. Her self-confidence, extroverted personality and enthusiasm drove her to success. As Mackie had realized, she exhibited unusual determination to create the life she desired.

She and Etha Cook attended Tacoma High School together. They graduated in 1912. Mr. Kay gave her a diamond ring for graduation. The ceremony celebrated the class's many talents. Etha, a gifted musician, played two piano numbers. Minnie read from *The Counsel Assigned,* a story about Lincoln as a lawyer. The *Tacoma Daily Ledger* reported:

> *Minnie McDowell captured the audience completely with her reading of "The Counsel Assigned," by Mary Shipman Andrews, which is a touching story of an incident in the life of Abraham Lincoln in which he volunteers his services as attorney for the boy of an old friend being tried for murder. Miss McDowell has a pleasantly modulated voice and she gave the reading with effective dignity and repose.*[1]

Minnie attended Whitworth College in Tacoma in the 1913-14 schoolyear. She and Etha shared a house where Etha taught piano. When the year ended, Whitworth moved their campus to Spokane, Washington, and she didn't continue. She would have graduated in 1917.

While at Whitworth, she was elected Freshman Class Historian. She wrote "Whitworth's Bequest" (the class legacy) in the yearbook as well as the Freshman Class History. Her typical enthusiasm surged from the page:

> *The history of the [class] of 1917 is up to date! One whose knowledge did not include [acquaintance] with this class might think that subject void of possibilities. But the reverse is true in this instance. The words call us a vision as pregnant with suggestive light and color as an impressionistic painting, a*

panorama of swiftly moving events, all showing the spirit and strength of this class. . . . We can only say that we believe the future. . . . will develop more class spirit in us, and promise that it will be turned into the general channel to swell the stream of school loyalty.[2]

Whitworth College Freshman class 1914. Minnie is in the second row, third from left. Item located in the Whitworth University Archives, Spokane, WA. Used with permission.

Minnie meets the man she will marry.

There is no energy unless there is a tension of opposites – Carl Jung

Minnie straightened up the living room in their small, shared house while Etha finished preparing the appetizers. She handed the tray to Minnie. "Here's the appetizer tray with salted nuts, olives and candied ginger."

"That looks delicious. I'll put it in the front room. I just finished cleaning." Minnie took the tray into the living room and put it on the small blue-and-white tile table between two overstuffed chairs. She pulled back the lace curtain and peered out the window.

"Oh, I hope we're ready," she called to Etha. "Our first guests are at the door right now." She rushed to the door and flung it open.

"Welcome. You're the first ones here."

"Good afternoon. I'm Frankie, a friend of Etha's. This is my friend, Karl."

"It's so nice to meet you both. Please come in. I'll take your coats." She waved them into the room as she took their coats and shut the door.

She smiled and looked at Karl. "Do you live around here, Karl?"

His eyes sparkled. He gave her a huge smile. "You can just call me Kling or KJK. Those are my nicknames. I live near Commencement Bay by the sawmills. I work there as a shingle sawyer. I work the night shift, so I can get up and go straight to work."

"Oh, really? That must be a good job. Do you work long hours?"

"It's a ten hour shift. What do you do?"

Minnie stood up straighter, raised an eyebrow and smiled. "I'm a student at Whitworth. I hope to teach someday. Etha and I are roommates. She teaches piano."

Kling nodded. "You're ambitious. That's great." He studied her face and looked deeply into her eyes. "What do you want to teach?"

She flashed him a smile. "I don't know yet – maybe something in speech or English."

He leaned forward and spread his arms in an animated gesture. "Wow! That's a great idea. You could help lots of students, I'll bet. Let's talk more later. Would you like to take a walk after we eat?"

She laughed. "I'd love to. I need to help Etha serve now; dinner's ready."

As she turned and walked away with their coats, Kling jabbed Frankie in the ribs. He leaned over and spoke in a low tone. "I didn't know you were going to introduce me to a woman that beautiful." He grinned. "Thanks, pal. I like her a lot. She's full of spunk."

Minnie smiled to herself as she walked to the bedroom with the coats and put them on the bed. She felt tingly all over. *Hmmm . . . he is handsome and interesting. And he's older. I like older men. He seems like fun and he's friendly too. I can't wait to get to know him better.*

1915–1922 – Everett and Seattle, Washington

Minnie and Kling marry.

The self I held dear last year is no more. Even memories change. New adventures are on the horizon.

Minnie didn't return to college because the school moved to Spokane. Her mother couldn't support her. Kling was fifteen years older, the same age difference that had been between her mother and T. J. She was attracted to him; he was smart, appealing, fun and mature. She saw the potential for a secure future. They were married by the Justice of the Peace in a civil ceremony in Everett, Washington on October 5, 1915. Etha and Frankie were their witnesses.

Everett, the "City of Smokestacks," was known as a union town. Labor disruptions and strikes were common. In 1914-15, an economic depression affected the region. The shingle weavers, who cut and packaged the cedar shingles, had a pay decrease. In 1916, shake prices rose and their union demanded a return to the former wage scale. Everett's mills did not comply the way other companies throughout the state had. Strikes and rallies resulted, culminating in a gun battle on November 5, 1916, between the Industrial Workers of the World (the IWW, or "Wobblies") and local law enforcement backed by citizen deputies. The result was several deaths and many wounded. This incident became known as the infamous Everett Massacre.[3]

In 1916, Kling and Minnie lived in Everett where he worked in the mills. Probably due to the continuing labor issues, they moved to Seattle after a couple of years, where he sold sewing machines. Minnie got pregnant right away. Twin boys were born in Everett on August 25, 1916. One died shortly after birth. She was heartbroken as any mother would be. It was Kling, though, who grieved profoundly. He later recalled: *I was so heartbroken when Jud died. I never got over it. We always called Donn by Jud's name. I had it legally changed to Judson years later just before he became twenty-one.*

Minnie recorded in her journal:

Sept. 23, 1916 – I lost a son. I must put my grief behind me now. I've grown stronger. My life is ahead.

After they moved to Seattle, they had two more children, the girls: Gail (my mother) was born in 1920, and Joyce in 1922.

1916–1920 – Seattle, Washington

Mackie rebounds with love of family and friends

All excellent things are as difficult as they are rare. – Benedict Spinoza

Mackie, after all her personal struggles and changes, had become settled by 1916. She'd moved to Seattle, where she ran another boarding house for workingmen. She and Ben (Mr. Kay) had divorced. She described her personal struggle this way:

I learned how to flow with the radical changes in my life and accept help from family and friends. I couldn't control circumstances. I could only control my thoughts and reactions. I'd always had faith; now, with all the kindness I received, my spirit expanded with love.

As I grew within myself, I understood that all things worth having are challenging. My faith, my ability to love and accept love, was the outcome of my struggle. I realized I could be happy with my life. I could say "yes" to life, accept what was, and be content in the present. I was fulfilled. I could come from the love in my soul. Love heals all. It's that simple. I learned to let the little things go. I practiced gratitude and turned my worries over to God.

Mackie met another wonderful man, Joseph Alexander Shock (originally Schock; he changed it after settling in Seattle), who became her husband in 1916. Joe had emigrated from Belgium in 1913 to find a better life. He was a successful sewing machine salesman, and they were able to buy two houses in Seattle. One of them Minnie eventually called her home in the Roosevelt District. The other was the house that Mackie and Joe enjoyed in Ballard.

Mackie and Joe were perfect for each other. She'd matured, overcome grief and hardship. She'd grown in faith and confidence. She emanated cheerfulness and love to everyone. Again, she was ready to move on. She later recalled when they met:

I met Joe through a friend and was immediately attracted to him. I was surprised that we were so alike. He demonstrated the same joy and love of life that I now felt in my heart. We became friends and very soon knew we were meant for each other. We had so much fun together. We were both optimistic about everything. Joe loved to laugh; he was a ray of sunshine to everyone. He was so buoyant and upbeat, always bringing joy to others.

His personality touched something in me that brought my ability to love to a new level. Our lives expanded with togetherness and love. We both enjoyed sharing the little things in life: a walk on the beach, a trip to our friend's mountain cabin or just being together at home. Our life and love enlarged with gratitude and joy in a way I had never imagined possible. My heart overflowed with happiness.

Joseph and Mackie Shock, c. 1920

Mother remembered Joe this way:

He's the grandfather I remember from my very early childhood. We called him "Daddy Joe." He had a strong Belgian accent – we loved to listen to him talk. He was a lot of fun. We loved him with a passion. He had one of those wonderful touring cars with the tool box on the running board and the isinglass windows. We used to play in it.

1920–1921 – Seattle, Washington

The Wayfarer – A religious pageant extraordinaire

I trust my higher power to work through me.

Historical and religious pageantry skyrocketed to popularity in the U.S. after World War I, reflecting post war sentiments of patriotism, religious fervor and nationalism/isolationism. Pageant-dramas presented in large venues stirred religious and patriotic feelings. They encouraged community participation and social reform through the re-creation of the life of Christ. This popular venue provided audiences with a unique experience of American patriotism, community pride, and religious duty as well as inexpensive family entertainment.

The Wayfarer, by Reverend James E. Crowther, was one of these pageants. It was presented at the University of Washington (UW) Stadium in Seattle from July 23–30, 1921. It became a featured annual event for several years. July is one of the warmest and sunniest months in Seattle. The flowers are showy, the air clear and Mt. Rainier visible; the perfect outdoor venue for a grand event.

The stadium seated 20,000. The pageant was presented for seven nights, and over 6,000 people assisted in making it a success. The seated chorus alone had 3,000 trained singers. Another 200 appeared onstage during the performance and 3,000 others participated in the episodes and the "March of Nations."[4]

Minnie, determined to be in the cast, was on her way to the auditions. She burst into the door of her mother's house.

"Oh, Mother, where are you?"

"In here. I'm in the kitchen."

Minnie's black T-strap shoes clattered on the floor as she rushed in. She carried Joyce on her hip and held Jud by the hand. He grasped Gail's hand firmly, pulling her along behind him.

"Mother, could you keep the children this afternoon? I have to go over to the UW." She handed Joyce to Mackie.

"Of course; I'd love to. What's going on over there today?"

Minnie pushed her hair off her face, straightened her glasses, patted her dark blue skirt with short strokes and turned sideways, striking a pose. "How do I look?"

"Well, beautiful as always. You're really excited. Why?"

"Oh Mother, this is the day I'm trying out for a part in *The Wayfarer.* I read about it in the *UW Daily.* It's going to be performed in the stadium. It's a passion play-drama with thousands of people in the cast. I'm sure I can get a part. I just feel it. Can you imagine, going to rehearsals, dressing in costume, and being on stage in the stadium? There's never been anything like it in Seattle. I'll find out today if I get the part. I'm trying out for one of the lead roles."

She fluffed her skirt, twisted a stray hair back from her face, threw her head back, and extended her arms dynamically. "I can see it now. I can feel it, Mother, how dramatic it will be, how exciting, just to be a part of a production so huge."

Mackie laughed her big laugh. "That's wonderful, McDowell. How exciting for you! I'm sure you'll get the part. And who knows where it could lead?"

"I know. I have to hurry and catch the streetcar. I'll see you soon. Good-bye Jud, Joyce and Gail. Here, give Momma a big kiss." She squeezed each of them in a warm hug. "Be good for your grandmother now. Momma will be back soon."

Later that night after she put the children to bed:

Minnie sat with her tea at the kitchen table, studying *The Wayfarer* booklet. Kling relaxed in his coffee-brown, soft-cushioned chair in the living room, engrossed in the *Seattle Daily Times.*

"Kling, you'll never guess what happened today." She looked over at him, smiling expectantly.

He continued reading. "Hmmm?"

"Put that down, would you please? I have something special to share." She bounded across the room, pulled up the footstool and sat down next to him. She rattled the newspaper with her finger. He looked up, annoyed. "What's the fuss all about?"

"I'm going to be in *The Wayfarer.* I got the part today. Can you believe it? Twenty-seven people tried out. They chose two actors for each of the three leading roles – we'll play on alternate nights. I'm going to play the character called *Understanding.* It's an important role, too." She held up the *Wayfarer* booklet and read, " '*Understanding* symbolizes the people whose faith in God and the goodness of life was shaken by war's tragedy. She is the divine messenger who guides the Wayfarer back to faith.' "[5]

She paused. "Isn't this is wonderful? What an opportunity! I'll be on stage in the UW Stadium."

"Oh, really? I saw something about it in the paper. How are you going to do that with three small children? I need you here. I want dinner when I come home, and lunches to take to the shop."

"Momma's going to help me. She'll watch them during rehearsals. Oh, Kling, it's such an opportunity for me. I'm so fortunate. Can you imagine? I'll be on stage with hundreds of people. Some well-known ones, too. The audience will be huge. The music will swell like a heavenly chorus, lifting their voices to majestic Mount Rainier. There will be thousands of singers in the choir alone. I'm so excited about this!"

"Well . . . ." He paused. "How will you maintain our home if you're never here? Who's going to cook? I know I'm not."

"It won't be all the time. We'll manage. I'll fix dinner in the morning, and your lunch too. Kling, this is my chance. I love drama, pageantry and costumes. It could open doors for me – opportunities I can't even imagine."

He sighed and looked down, dropping the newspaper on the table. "Well, I hope it doesn't change our schedule too much. I'll be at the shop all day. We've been pretty busy lately. But if you really want to do it, I suppose it's okay."

She reached over and threw her arms around him. "I'm so happy!"

She wrote in her journal that evening:

June 9, 1921 – This is what I've waited for; an opportunity of a lifetime. It will be breathtaking.

Minnie in The Wayfarer, 1921 (2, center top) University of Washington Libraries, Special Collections, UW37868.

3 ~ Positive Intention and Faith Create Results

Whatever you put your attention on will grow stronger in your life.
– Deepak Chopra

1921–1922 – Seattle, Washington

Education, key to the future

When you evoke the emotions of what you desire, you move through the space-time continuum to create your dream.

After her experience in *The Wayfarer*, Minnie recognized where she was headed. She saw her potential in dramatic art and teaching. She'd grown in confidence and felt her positive energy surge when she auditioned for the role. Intuitively, it felt right. She had matured, she'd known loss and learned to make hard decisions. She sensed her internal guidance.

She knew she needed more education. Seattle's Cornish School (now Cornish College of the Arts) was the perfect option. Founded by Nellie Cornish in 1914 as Cornish School of Music, it expanded into Cornish School in 1920 with art, drama and dance. It was the perfect venue for an aspiring actress and teacher.

After dinner, and after she'd put the children to bed, Minnie curled up in the cushy brown chair by the window. Light filtered in through the filmy curtains. She tucked her brightly patterned skirt under her and opened the *Cornish School Catalog*. Kling sat on the sofa, perusing the *Seattle Daily Times*, his evening relaxation.

She glanced over at him tentatively. "How's it going at the shop?"

"Pretty well." He set the paper in his lap. "I sold a couple of the new Singer sewing machines this week. It's hard to tell though. More women are buying readymade clothing because they work and don't have time to sew."

She flashed him an encouraging smile. "Well, I'm glad you're selling some. I hope it keeps up and you do really well this year." She paused, ruffling the pages of the catalog. She spoke deliberately. "Kling, I want to talk to you. I'm thinking about going back to school."

His mouth fell open as he stared at her incredulously. "What? How can you do that with the children? We just got through *The Wayfarer*. They need you here. They're still so young. Joyce is only sixteen months old, Gail is three and Jud is five. How could you leave them? What about the money? We can't afford it." His voice escalated. "It's absolutely out of the question." He scowled and slammed his fist into the sofa arm.

She eyed him intently, studying his eyes and expression. She'd become used to his outbursts. She continued calmly, "I talked to Mother. She will help us. I want to enroll in Cornish School. They have a wonderful curriculum in the arts and I could get the education I need to be able to teach. I'm going to look into it. Being in *The Wayfarer* made me realize that opportunities exist that I didn't know about. Kling, I really want to do this."

He picked up the newspaper abruptly and shoved it onto the dark walnut coffee table. He knit his brows and frowned. His mouth hardened into a straight line while he stared past her at the wall.

He glanced at her coldly. His nostrils flared. He spoke with a controlled tone. "I don't see how you can. You have a household to take care of. The children need you and so do I. You know I can't work and take care of the house, too. I work hard whether I'm in the mill or at the shop. We can't afford this. You're too stubborn and self-centered. You need to think about the family more, and about me. What happened to what *we* want?"

She sat up straight. Her eyes widened. "I haven't forgotten. In fact that's one of my reasons. If I work, we can support the family together. Mother will care for the children. She has the time. She loves taking care of them. School is only part time. I can schedule classes around your schedule and hers."

Kling sat back and crossed his arms. "Where's the money coming from? You know we've been struggling."

Minnie stretched her arms and held her hands open in a wide gesture. "Mother will help us. She already told me she would. Joe is doing really well in his sales business; he travels all over. And we can make payments to the school too."

He shook his head. "You have all the answers, don't you?" He got up, picked up the newspaper, threw it on the couch and paced around the room, staring at the floor. He stopped, looked at her and threw his hands up. "I don't understand you. You always want more. You're never satisfied."

She looked up at him, her eyes pleading. Her voice softened. "Think about our future. Together we can support the family the way we want to. We'll have more opportunities. So will the children. It's our future and our children's future I'm considering. Schooling is an investment that never ends. Think about it, Kling."

He stared at her intently, perched on the edge of the couch and shook his head. He took a deep breath, and sighed loudly. "Well, I guess so. If your mother can help us, it would be feasible."

"Oh, I know it is. It's an opportunity we'll never regret."

"I hope not." Kling looked down, picked up the paper again and collapsed heavily onto the couch.

Minnie enrolled in Cornish School for the 1921–22 schoolyear in *The School of the Spoken Word.* She studied the English literature curriculum (Classic, Romanic and Modern styles), which included mastery of the techniques of speech, expression, impersonation, pantomime and oratory as well as sight reading, analyzing passages of literature, and reciting them from memory. She graduated in April 1922 in the first class of this new Cornish division.

1922–1926 – Hoquiam, Washington

A new drama unfolds.

Create the image and emotions, surround it with pink light and love; release it. Give up "hope." You should feel like you'll never have it. This process is a link between us and the creative forces of the Universe.

The Klingbergs moved to Hoquiam, Washington around 1922–23. They later relocated to its sister city across the river, Aberdeen. It was another move to bolster Kling's income. Grays Harbor, on the Olympic Peninsula, was one of the prime timber locations in Washington State. He'd be able to use his skill as a sawyer again in the shingle mills. This was his lifetime trade. It was hard and dangerous work. Washington State's *History Link* describes the mills:

> *Shingle mills were highly dangerous places. Workers usually put in 10-hour shifts, and early twentieth-century technology brought machines that were designed for efficient production, not safety. Unshielded saws ran fast and the mill interiors were dark and damp. Accidents were common, and it was said that a shingle worker could be identified by his missing digits. Some lost their lives in accidents, but more fell victim to cedar dust. As cedar was cut, sawdust rose in clouds and filled workers' lungs, causing a condition commonly referred to as "cedar asthma." For many, this led to a slow and agonizing death.*[6]

The family rented an apartment on the second floor of the Lytle Building in the middle of booming downtown Hoquiam (the 1920 population was 10,000). My mother recalled it in her life story:

> *In Hoquiam we lived in an apartment above a furniture store, right downtown. It was known as the Lytle-Bitar Block. I remember lying in bed at night and seeing light reflections flash across the bedroom ceiling from cars going by. And yet at the same time there was the clumping sound of horses' hooves. It was the beginning of an era of change.*

The Lytle Block, c. 1926.
Courtesy of the Polson Museum, Hoquiam, WA

Minnie reinvented herself and put her new skills to work. She listed herself in the Hoquiam City Business Directory as an "elocutionist." Elocution is the art of public speaking in which voice, pronunciation, gesture, and delivery are emphasized. She gave private drama and speaking lessons in their apartment. This began her tradition of teaching in her home, which she continued for the rest of her career.

She gave public readings at libraries, local drama events and for charities, and became a well-known interpretive reader in the area. She advertised her services as an instructor in dramatic art in the Weatherwax High School newspaper.[7] She also began using her maiden name as her professional name. From this time on, she was known to her students as "Miss McDowell."

In 1924, she started working part-time at Weatherwax High School and coached the senior play. The following year, she was one of three drama coaches for the senior play.

Minnie began attending the UW in Seattle during the summers to get her B.A. and teaching credential. She knew she needed a degree and certification to teach full time, and worked toward this goal for several years. She took the girls with her every summer; they stayed with Mackie. Kling stayed in Aberdeen or Hoquiam to work, and Jud lived with him.

The Klingberg family, c. 1926
L to R - Minnie, Kling, Joyce, Gail, Jud

1920–1926 – Seattle (Ballard District), Washington

Mackie's faith grows.

If you have trouble letting go, you lack true faith.

While Minnie pursued her education and career, her mother strengthened her faith and began attending the Christian Science Church.

On a typical breezy, misty Sunday afternoon, Mackie and Mary, whom she'd known in Grays Harbor while growing up, arrived home from the Second Church of Christ, Scientist, in Ballard. Mackie opened the door and they stepped inside. She set her black-leather clutch purse on the entry table. She took off her coat, hung it in the closet and smoothed the pleats of her tan, calf-length skirt. "Just put your things here." She motioned to the table and a nearby chair. "Come in. Let's sit in the parlor."

Mary set her things down and followed Mackie inside. "Your house always smells so good, like you've just baked something delicious. It smells like the homes we grew up in. I'm glad John and I moved to

Seattle, though. There are so many more opportunities here for both work and church."

Mackie laughed. "I agree. I'm happy to be here, too. I haven't baked today, but I have chocolate cake left from last week. I'll bring it out and fix some tea." She stepped into the kitchen. "I enjoyed the Bible lesson sermon today. It was uplifting. Friends introduced me to Christian Science a while ago. It appeals to me because it's based on the Bible. When I can't attend church, I always stop by to pick up the latest literature."

Mackie brought out cups of hot tea and slices of chocolate cake. She set them on the table and sat down.

Mary said, "I enjoyed the service too. How did Christian Science start?"

"The Christian Science Church was founded by Mary Baker Eddy in 1879. Mrs. Eddy healed herself from a fall on the ice in 1866 when she read Matthew 9:2: *And behold, they were bringing to him a paralytic, lying on a bed, and Jesus seeing their faith said to the paralytic, 'Take courage, My son, your sins are forgiven.'* "

Mackie continued, "Mrs. Eddy devoted the next three years of her life to studying scripture and she discovered what she considered the principles of healing as Jesus did. Her book, *Science and Health with Key to the Scriptures,* was first published in 1875. In it, she says that prayer, unselfish love and spiritual understanding of God heal the sick and reform sinners."[8]

"That's very hopeful. I need more spiritual understanding. I'm worried because John is out of work again. He had a good job, but the business closed. We're not getting along well and we're struggling with finances. He doesn't stay home much. I suspect he's hanging out with some friends at a speakeasy and drinking. I smell it on his breath when he comes home in the evening.

"I've lost my faith. I'm discouraged, and I know John is too. How do you always seem so happy and buoyant? I know you have Joe, and he's a wonderful man. He's clever, and he prospers in anything he does. You're so fortunate. You don't seem to have any problems."

Mackie smiled. "Oh, I don't know. I'm grateful to be happy now. When T. J. died, I was crushed. I was alone, and I had to find a way to support myself and Minnie. I realized that faith is always the key. I turned to God to help me overcome my fear and loss. I leaned on God and realized that I was guided.

"I learned that mind, not flesh and blood, guides our actions. Spirit moves through our souls into our lives in everything we think and do, whether we realize it or not. Mrs. Eddy says that Spirit is real and eternal. Spirit is God, and we are His image and likeness; therefore, we're not material. We are part of the mind of God and can't be otherwise. She says we must form perfect models in thought and keep with those thoughts continually to create them in our lives."[9]

"I love that; it's so encouraging. Your love and resilience are an inspiration, Mackie. I still struggle with faith."

"You're not alone. Even if you lapse in your faith – which you will – you can come back stronger. Let it be a way to increase your faith, your strength, and your compassion for your husband. Put your faith in God. You can't control your husband's moods or actions. Just come from love. He'll feel it. It will encourage him, and it will transform your relationship, too. He will find work. Pray about it. Know that God's will is good – He loves us, and we can rely on that. Faith and love create powerful results if we just let them into our hearts and minds."

"Thank you so much." She leaned towards Mackie, parted her lips and let out her breath easily. "I feel lighter now. Your love shines through you. Thank you so much for talking with me. My mood is uplifted. I feel hopeful again."

Mackie reached across the table and squeezed Mary's hand affectionately. She smiled broadly. "You're welcome. We're all in this together, and we can help each other. I'll see you in church next week. Why don't you bring John? It would be nice to see him again. Maybe he could find some friends at the social. You're a strong woman, Mary. Your faith will grow again if you hold the right thought."

4 ~ Build Resilience

There is no higher drama than true personal growth.
– Marianne Williamson

1926 – Aberdeen, Washington

Practice, practice, practice!

Imagine and create your power.

In her teaching career at Weatherwax High, Minnie became the director of numerous productions. One of the most outstanding was the annual senior play. She held rehearsals both at school and at her home.

It's play rehearsal night at the Klingberg-McDowell home. *The Goose Hangs High* by Lewis Beach is the Weatherwax High senior play this year. The Quinault yearbook tells us it's about "a present-day problem that confronts parents of college students."[10]

In the play, a middle-class family has sacrificed to send their three children to college and provide for their every need. The students, home for the holidays, are ready to party (to their parents' dismay) but when a financial crisis looms, they surprise their parents by willingly stepping up to help.

The living room is crowded. Students sit on every available chair, stand along the walls or lounge on the rug. Miss McDowell directs the cast.

"Let's start with Act III tonight, where the conflict must be resolved. The father, Bernard, resigned his position as city accountant in a fit of anger, because of a political maneuver by a city council member who threatened to fire him. With no income, their three children cannot return to college after Christmas break. Bernard agonized over the crisis

"The Entrance," by Ben K. Weatherwax, 1927. WHS Quinault yearbook. Courtesy of the Polson Museum, Hoquiam, WA

and decided what to do. Unknown to him, his wife, Eunice, and the children (Hugh, Lois, and Bradley), conspired together to initiate different solutions. The scene opens when Hugh wants to give his father back the check intended to pay for next semester's schooling, because now it's needed to pay the rent.

"Let's start with Bernard – Raymond, that's your part. Imagine how you would feel if you were Bernard, the father. You've just lost your job. Maybe you shouldn't have argued with the councilman. You're ashamed and worried, but you've decided what you need to do. Go ahead, Raymond. Imagine the scene first, and then read."

Raymond stood up, script in hand. He started to read, " 'Silence! All of you!' "

Miss McDowell interrupted. "Cut. Now take a deep breath and clear your throat. Put emotion into your voice. This man is unemployed. He's proud. He won't take back the check he wrote for his eldest son's schooling, even though he's desperate. He's confused, worried. Imagine it. Feel it. Put more expression into your voice. You are Bernard; you're feeling his agony in this role. Magnify his feelings. Project the emotion; let it flow out of you. Start again, please."

Raymond took a deep breath, cleared his throat and read. The voice that came out roared more powerfully than any sound he'd ever made.

" 'Silence! All of you! If you think you're going to run things here you're sadly mistaken. A lot of nerve you had, doing what you've done without my permission. But I still am boss.' "[11]

Everyone clapped.

"That's it, Raymond. You got it! You projected your emotion to the audience. Did all of you feel how angry and upset he was?"

A chorus of "Yes we did. It was powerful. Good job," came from the students.

"That's your power – for the audience to feel your emotion, to be there in the scene with you and experience your feelings. That's how you command the stage."

Minnie was an exacting professional. Her high standards propelled her students to success. With her infectious enthusiasm, her determination and the personal pride she took in training her students, she rapidly became well-known. She directed plays and coached students for Shakespearean contests, speeches and other venues. She put Weatherwax High School on the map as having one of the finest dramatics departments in the state. Her students won numerous awards in statewide speaking competitions. Although she was a perfectionist, she was well-loved.

One of her first students recalled her:

> *"Momma" Minnie was a director to be reckoned with. She was power personified. She used to say "practice makes perfect," and she really meant it.*
>
> *She got the very best out of us and it all came from love – her love of her students and the theatre. She was a hard taskmaster. She expected perfection and she got it repeatedly. We all loved her. She somehow commanded love, too. You couldn't* not *love her. Her personality was big. Her love was big. When she strode into a room or onto the stage, she commanded the space. She knew who she was and she let you know it too. We'd do just about anything for her. Her love, which she used to push us to be our best, to make each of us stars in our own way, was her method. She taught by example. She was totally passionate about helping others through the theatre. That's how her amazing productions were created. She never failed.*

September 12, 1926 – Oakland, California and Seattle (Ballard District), Washington

Faith is the key.

I believe, trust, and have faith.

Mackie happily continued her life with Joe, enjoyed having Minnie and the girls stay during the summers, and attended church with her many friends.

Mackie and Anna walk home from the Second Church of Christ, Scientist, in Ballard, on a sunny, spring afternoon. The trees are blooming; pink and white blossoms cover the ground, blown off by blustery wind earlier that day. Daffodils spread their brilliant yellow blanket over the gardens they pass.

"Mackie, won't you come in? We'll sit and visit before lunch." Anna held the door open.

"Thank you, Anna, I'd love to. I have time before Joe gets home. I enjoy visiting with you. I'm glad we met at the church social last month."

"So am I. It's uplifting to have like-minded friends. Please sit down." Anna motioned to the dining-room table and chairs. "I'll pour us some iced tea." She set her Bible and the *Christian Science Quarterly* on the table. "The readings today inspired me. I love this passage." She picked up the *Quarterly* and read: " 'Spirit is the only substance, the invisible and indivisible infinite God. Things spiritual and eternal are substantial. Things material and temporal are insubstantial. In Christian Science, substance is understood to be Spirit.' "[12]

"I agree," Mackie said as she sipped her tea. "I especially love the Biblical reference to Hebrews 11:1: *Now faith is the assurance of things hoped for, the conviction of things not seen.*"

Mackie continued, "Today's lesson referred to this scripture, and reminded us that love, life and truth are substance.[13] I've been studying Christian Science for a while. It really strikes a chord within me. I love the emphasis on spirituality. I believe it's important to focus on the spiritual more and on the material world less. Love and spirit are the primary laws of life, and they reflect God's actions through us. It's so uplifting."

Anna nodded. "The readings always motivate me to read and study more. Mrs. Eddy revised her book until her death in 1910, so her ideas are still quite new."

Mackie finished her tea. "I'm very happy I found Christian Science. Let's talk more next Sunday. I'd better get home now. Joe will be ready for lunch. Thank you for the tea." She picked up her Bible and purse.

Anna accompanied her to the door. "Thanks for stopping by to visit, Mackie. Tell Joe hello for me."

"I will. See you next Sunday."

Mackie walked home leisurely, enjoying the sun, the shadows cast by the trees, and the red and white tulips in neat beds along the sidewalks. She walked up the front stairs. Joe was sitting on the porch, waiting.

"Mackie, you look so lovely in your purple taffeta dress and hat."

She bent down and kissed his cheek. "Thank you my dear. It's my spring outfit. You're always so sweet. Are you ready for lunch?"

"Yes." He got up and swung the door open for her. "You know I have to go to California on business tomorrow."

"Oh? I didn't know. Did you mention that?"

"I think so. I need to meet with the managers of some larger White Sewing Machine stores. I'll be gone at least a week."

"Oh, I'll miss you."

"I'll miss you too. Let's do something special together when I get back. The weather's unusually warm and sunny. We could go for a drive or to Golden Gardens for a picnic."

"I always love to go there. Hurry back." She laughed and gave him a hug. He held her tenderly in his arms, nuzzling his face into her neck and hair.

"You know I love you so much," he whispered.

They turned facing each other, smiling. Their eyes opened wider and met in a loving gaze. He bent toward her, touching her lips with his, gently caressing them. She responded, pulling his lips into hers, relishing his taste and scent. They held each other for a moment longer. Then he held her away from him, and looked lovingly into her eyes.

"I can't wait to come home. I'm so happy we found each other. This is the best time of our lives."

She laughed and squeezed him tightly in a warm hug. He responded enthusiastically, holding her close. "I love you too," she said tenderly.

"You've brought so much love, laughter and joy into my life. More than I ever imagined possible."

"You have for me too. Let's have lunch and spend the afternoon together. I'll leave in the morning."

She smiled, caressing him with her eyes while she squeezed his hand. "I'll fix lunch and we'll have a wonderful afternoon together. I'll help you pack tonight."

September 24, 1926 – Oakland, California and Seattle (Ballard District), Washington

Change – the only constant

I'm trapped on the karmic wheel. My emotions are turning, churning; change overcomes me.

Mackie sat alone in the parlor, reading. The phone rang.

"Good afternoon."

"Is this Mrs. Joseph Shock?"

"Yes it is."

"Mrs. Shock, this is Dr. Sutherland at Fabiola Hospital in Oakland, California. I have sad news for you. Your husband, Joseph, passed away in our hospital. He died of cerebral apoplexy [a stroke]. His high blood pressure was undoubtedly a contributing factor. I am so sorry. I know you are far away in Seattle. I deeply regret having to call you and give you this heartbreaking news."

Mackie gasped. *Not again.*

"What? Did I hear you right? Joe died in the hospital? There wasn't anything wrong with him. He was fine when he left a week ago."

"I'm sorry, Mrs. Shock. He probably had high blood pressure and didn't know. There may not be any symptoms."

She stuttered, "I . . . I can't believe it." A sob caught in her throat. She sat down at the table and moaned softly. "Oh, this can't be true." She started sobbing into the phone.

"Mrs. Shock, please calm down. Just wait a moment; I'll have one of our nurses help you. She can give you more information so you can make arrangements."

"Yes." Tears flowed down her face. "Yes, I'll wait."

Mackie put the phone down and pulled her blue sweater around her, burying her face in the collar and wiping her tears. *No, not again. I've lost the love of my life again. Why, God, why? What am I going to do?*

Dazed, she stared at the floor. She barely heard the nurse talking to her. She answered the questions, made cremation arrangements. But she was hardly able to think. All she could feel was a vacant numbness overcoming her mind, heart and body. She put down the phone, slumped into the chair and pressed her hands against her chest. She stared out the window, but her blurry eyes saw nothing. Her chin trembled. She shivered, moaned and choked out another sob. The aching depth of sorrow in her heart overtook her once again.

Later, she later recalled her experience and how she grew from it despite her sorrow:

I was devastated by Joe's death because I was so sure my life had changed in wonderful ways that wouldn't change again. But the unexpected happened. I knew what I had to do after Joe died. I didn't really know much about his business, but I knew he had clients everywhere. A friend advised me to put a notice in the paper about his death, so I did.

He provided well for me. I had both houses. One was rented, and I already had boarders in our home so that wasn't a problem. It was just business. But for my heart it wasn't. I was alone and heartbroken once again. I had to find a way through my grief, but I didn't know how.

5 ~ Pursue Personal Growth

I'm tough. I'm ambitious, and I know exactly what I want.
If that makes me a bitch, okay. – Madonna

1929–1932 – Aberdeen, Washington – The Klingberg-McDowell home

A family at stake

Go for it now. The future is promised to no one. – Wayne Dyer

At Weatherwax High, Minnie continued teaching and directing high school productions. A boisterous group of high school theatre students has just left after the evening's senior play rehearsal at her home. Chairs are still scattered around the living room; some copies of the script have spilled over from a stack on the floor. A few dirty plates and napkins are strewn around also: some on chairs, others on the floor. Jud, Gail and Joyce have disappeared to their rooms for the night.

Kling sat at the worn, wooden kitchen table, having a hot cup of coffee before leaving for his shift at the mill. A steady, beating rain hit the window with relentless tapping. Dampness held its grip on the house. Minnie packed his lunch at the counter, her back to him.

He sat pensively, hands grasping his cup, enjoying the warmth of the hot coffee. He looked up and stared at Minnie's back. "You know, it would be a lot more peaceful and quiet around here if you just had your play rehearsals at school. Why don't you?"

She busily continued preparing his lunch. "We usually do. This is just more convenient. I can be at home, everyone can go home from school, do their homework and chores, have a bite to eat and then come over here."

"Yes, and sometimes they stay for dinner too. You invite them. How do you think I can support a household of high school students for dinner a couple of nights a week?

She laughed, turned and glanced at him quickly. "It isn't that often. I don't think it's a problem. I contribute to the family income too. Sometimes it's just easier to do it here. They can talk about the play, and I can give them more direction in an informal way. It's a win-win for everyone."

"Not for me, it isn't. I sleep during the day, get up in the afternoon and I'd like some time alone with the family or just to relax in the evening before I go to work. Is that asking too much? I don't think so."

"No, of course not." She turned to him, wiping her hands on her stained apron. She stared at him, pressed her lips together and spoke slowly. "You have to realize I have my duties too. Part of that is to help these kids be the best they can be."

Kling returned her steady gaze. "What about *our* children? They deserve your time too. *They* deserve to be the best."

She put her hands on her hips and took a step forward. Her apron brushed against the worn edge of the table. She spoke firmly. "I see them at school every day. They're in my homeroom. We have plenty of time together in the evenings too. I don't know what you're talking about."

He sat back in his chair, tipping it into the wall. He cracked his knuckles and folded his arms across his chest. "Well, that's not family time. We should spend more time at home together. If you didn't spend so much time with your students, you could take better care of *our* children, cook regularly, and save money. You act like you don't even care about our family."

She extended her arms in a wide gesture, tilted her head and rolled her eyes. "How can you say that? Of course I care. I'm employed. Teaching is more than just showing up at school every day. It's a commitment. You don't understand that. You don't really spend any time with them yourself. How can you accuse me of not doing that? When you're here during the day, we're all at school. Sometimes in the late afternoon you go out with the men you work with. You're always over at Harry's, talking about work, wages, the unions, possible strikes, but resolving nothing. You could be at home with them too, you know."

Kling threw his arms into the air and raised his voice. His arms quivered. "Damn it! I need time to relax without a house full of teenagers. I work ten-hour shifts. The saws are constantly spinning. It's fast-paced, dangerous work. I have to be alert all the time. One slip of my hand and I could lose it. I'm fortunate to be skilled and able to work. You don't care about that. He slammed his fist on the table, knocking over his coffee. He stood up abruptly, shoving the battered chair against the wall.

Minnie turned back to the counter, put his sandwiches in the bag and folded it. She picked it up and turned to face him. She lifted her chin and looked into his eyes. She spoke quietly. "I do care. I have stress at my job, too. I'm doing the best I can." She set the bag on the table. She wiped her hands on her apron. "I think we've grown apart. We've both changed. We don't understand each other anymore." She gestured at the bag. "Here's your lunch," she said softly. "Have a safe shift. Rehearsals are at school tomorrow so it will be quiet here. I need to correct some papers now. See you tomorrow."

He snapped, "You don't give a damn about us at all! It's all about you, your career, your success." He picked up the coffee cup, set it in the sink, and wiped the spilled coffee from the table in silence. He tucked in his faded black-and-gray-checked flannel shirt, picked up his lunch bag and turned toward the door. He put on his jacket and hat and walked out into the rain, slamming the door behind him.

1932 – Aberdeen, Washington

Gail's usual shopping trip results in the unexpected.

I need to have patience with myself and my situation.

Gail was the oldest girl and Minnie's helper. At fourteen, she often walked to the store on the way home from school to pick up groceries for dinner. She started dinner so Minnie could finish it quickly when she arrived home late from school.

It was the end of a typical school day. Fifth period was over, and Gail had stayed after school to study with her friend. She closed her textbook and looked up. "Well, Helen, I'm glad we could do our history homework together. It was fun. We got it done fast, too."

"I'm happy too. Now we won't have to do it tonight. See you tomorrow." Helen grabbed her coat and books and turned toward the classroom door.

Gail put her books away and threw her coat over her arm. *I'd better get going. I have to get groceries, go home and start dinner. Momma will be late today. Too bad the cast isn't coming over tonight. Oh well, at least it will be quiet for a change.* She went out the side door, and started walking downtown. She passed businesses, cars, and people walking by on the sidewalk. It was a busy afternoon. *I wonder what's going on today. So many people are out.* She got to the store, pulled open the door and entered.

"Hi Bud, how are you?"

"Just fine, Gail. How about you?"

She nodded. "Oh, I'm all right. I have to get some groceries for Momma." She paused and looked around. *I don't remember what to get.* She gazed at the stacks of cans and groceries on the shelves behind the counter. *Oh, I remember now.* "I need two cans of pork and beans, two of corn, and a can of peaches."

"Sure, I'll get that right away." Bud smiled.

"Thanks." She waited at the counter while he got the items and put them in her bag. Suddenly, she started to feel queasy. She fidgeted with her coat. *I wonder what's wrong.* Bud handed her the bag and she paid him. *I don't feel well, I'd better get home.* She felt hot and dizzy. She grabbed the bag and headed abruptly for the door.

As she stepped out onto the street, a shadow suddenly crossed the doorway, startling her. She jumped back instinctively. Her heart beat faster. *What was that?* She looked around but didn't see anything unusual. *Why am I so scared? I can't breathe.* She clutched the bag, shifted her coat to her other arm and steadied herself against the doorway.

People walked past, cars drove by. She gulped to catch her breath. She stepped out into the gray late afternoon, hesitating. A wave of nausea overcame her, moving up from her stomach to her throat. Her chest tightened and panic gripped her. *What's happening to me? Am I going to die right here on the sidewalk?*

She grabbed the bag tightly and leaned against the wall. Another wave of nausea passed through her stomach. Terror paralyzed her. *I have to get home fast.* She forced herself to start walking, gripping the bag tightly to her chest. Head down, she walked as fast as she could, dodging people as they passed her. She started to cry softly. Finally, her breathing slowed, but her stomach still hurt. Her arms and chest became clammy. *I'm almost there – only a block farther.*

She ran the last block, opened the door, rushed to the kitchen and dropped the bag on the counter. She burst into tears and dashed into her room, slamming the door. *I'm so glad no one's here.* She threw herself onto the bed, gasping for air and sobbing into the pillow. She could breathe normally now. She slowly sat up, wiped her face and slumped onto the bed again. She felt exhausted. She reached for her journal, grabbed a pen and started to write.

> *Today I went to the store and something terrible happened. What's wrong with me? I got scared for no reason. Bud at the store was nice and helped me. First I forgot what Momma wanted, then I felt strange. I ran partway home. This never happened before. Now I'm afraid to go out of the house. Maybe it will happen again. I don't dare tell Momma. She won't listen. She never has time for me anyway. She'll say I'm making it up or tell me to just think the right thought and I'll be fine. I don't know what to do.*

She closed the journal softly and shoved it under a pile of books and clothing. *I don't want anyone to see this. They might think I'm weird. Maybe it won't happen again.* She jumped up quickly. *Oh, I have to start dinner. Momma and Joyce will be home soon.*

Years later, Mother recounted her first panic attack in her life story:

> *Sometimes Minnie was home late for cooking dinner, and if so I would start the dinner. It wasn't the habit in those days to buy a week's groceries at once – especially if you had to walk to town to buy the food and carry it many blocks home. So I used to walk to town after school to buy the food for dinner. It was on one of these trips to town when I was fourteen years old and a sophomore that I had my first panic attack – it was the beginning of life-long agoraphobia.*

In 1932, medical science didn't have sufficient knowledge of anxiety and panic attacks, nor the medications to treat them. It took half a century to understand anxiety better and develop appropriate medications. Fluoxetine (Prozac), an antidepressant selective serotonin reuptake inhibitor (SSRI) which effectively treats panic disorder and depression, was approved by the FDA in 1987.[14]

1930–1932 – Aberdeen, Washington

Minnie perseveres in her education and quest for a better job.

I materialize my dreams step by step. Creation occurs as I make my dreams real in the physical world.

Minnie attended the UW during the summers to get her undergraduate degree and teaching certificate. Her journal entries succinctly reveal her success:

> *January 21, 1930 – Got transcript of grades from U. I was graduated Dec. 20, 1929. Normal [teaching] diploma (5 year) also.*

> *Feb. 20, 1930 – Got A.B. [Bachelor of Arts] diploma from Univ. Good-looking blue leather case. Children all want one, too.*

> *Feb. 21, 1930 – Received 5-year Normal diploma. "A diploma a day" the youngsters remark.*

> *April 18, 1930 – Got word of my election to Phi Beta Kappa this morn. Am surprised and delighted. Children all impressed.*

She had worked hard for several years to obtain her degree. Her B.A. degree was granted in her married name, Klingberg. She wanted the degree granted in her professional name, Minnie Moore McDowell. She called her attorney, Matthew Hill. They'd been high school classmates.

Minnie "the Educator" with friends, c. 1932

"Hello, Matt. This is Minnie. How've you been? How's your law business doing?"

"Hi, Minnie. It's doing well, thanks. Did you finish your degree yet?"

"Yes. That's why I'm calling. I graduated and they issued the degree in my married name. I couldn't believe it because I specifically requested that it be issued in my professional name."

"That's not a problem. We can go to court. I'll draw up the papers this week."

"Thanks. I can't have a degree hanging in my office unless it has my professional name on it. Everyone at school and in the drama community knows me as Minnie Moore McDowell."

"Don't worry, I'll handle it."

"Great. Thanks again. I'll talk to you soon."

Matthew Hill represented her in court and her name was legally changed.

Minnie had been teaching part time without a contract. With her degree and diploma, the school district offered her a full-time position. That had been her goal in obtaining her additional education. She also started teaching at the local junior college. A friend advised her to try for a job in the Seattle schools, but that would come later.

Minnie was a feminist and a professional. She also had a strong sense of self, knew the value of branding and of having a stage name. It was obvious to her that her degree should have her professional name on it. Even so, her request to change her name was unusual for her time. She later recalled,

> *I'd been acting and speaking professionally since my role in "The Wayfarer" in 1921, and teaching since 1923. I was well-known in the Grays Harbor area and had many friends in Seattle and at the UW who were involved in the theater. I anticipated that I would eventually live in Seattle and become part of the local theatre there. I'd used my professional name since I started teaching, so that name needed to be on my academic degree.*

Many women obtained degrees when I did – my classes were full of them. I pursued my degree for the same reasons that most people do: to improve my relative standing in my field, be competitive for better job opportunities, and to expand my knowledge and gain credibility. It made sense to have my degree granted in my professional name.

The Seattle Times wryly commented on her victory:

Wife Discards Husband's Name for Sake Of Art; Court Sanctions Euphony Idea

K. L. KLINGBERG of Aberdeen, still has a wife, but henceforth she is going to be known as Minnie Moore McDowell. And if either one of them rue it—they say they won't—they cañ thank higher education.

Mrs. Klingberg appeared before Superior Judge Adam Beeler yesterday and requested the change of name. She explained that she was a music and dramatic teacher and amateur actress in her way and that the name of Minnie Moore McDowell formed more easily in the mouth than the less euphonious "Mrs. K. L. Klingberg."

It further appeared that Mrs. Klingberg has been attending summer school at the University of Washington this quarter and the University refused to grant a diploma to "Minnie Moore McDowell" when she was in reality Mrs. K. L. Klingberg, art or no art.

"And how," sighed Mrs. Klingberg, "could I show a diploma for Mrs. Klingberg to my artistic friends and students who know me as Minnie Moore McDowell?".

"How, indeed," agreed her attorney Matt Hill, "without appealing to the courts?"

So Judge Adam Beeler signed his name to a mere scrap of paper yesterday, and Mrs. Klingberg became euphonious.

The Sunday Times, July 28, 1929, p. 7. Copyright 1929, Seattle Times Company. Used with permission.

6 ~ Genuine Belief Creates and Heals

Faith is an affirmative mental approach to reality.
– Ernest Holmes

1929–1932 continued – Aberdeen and Seattle, Washington

Metamorphosis of a family

Opportunities to find deeper powers within ourselves come when life seems most challenging. – Joseph Campbell

Change percolated through the lumber industry, the area, and the family. The stock market crashed on October 24, 1929, ushering in the Great Depression. Minnie later recorded in her journal:

> *July 1, 1930 – Kling home. Mill shut down. Much talk of hard times, even panic, on all sides.*

They'd grown apart. Now Kling was out of work, too. Minnie became the sole support of the family for over a year. She wrote:

> *June 13, 1931 – Definitely made up my mind to get divorce and make a try for a bigger job. Can't send children to college on this one.*

> *June 14, 1931 – Kling opposed to divorce but will not contest it. Willing for me to have my "chance" as he calls it. Says I'm doing it for personal ambition.*

Their divorce was final on August 13, 1931. Jud was fifteen, Gail thirteen and Joyce eleven. Minnie retained custody of the children. Her maiden name was restored. Kling paid child support of $45 per month starting January 1932. The family was split for practical reasons. Jud lived with Kling in a two-story house at 500 I street in Aberdeen, most likely a shared residence. The girls stayed with her.

Kling was angry about the divorce. Her actions seemed completely self-centered to him. The qualities that had attracted him to her in the beginning – spunk, ambition, determination – had intensified over time. Her feelings had changed, too. He was no longer an interesting, sophisticated older man. With her passion for education and helping others, she'd outgrown him in education and personal growth, thrusting them farther apart.

Kling's attitude eventually changed and they became friends. More than likely he still felt angry over his own upbringing. His father was an old-country Swede who remarried after his mother died early in his childhood. Kling and his sister, Ellen, came west from Minnesota to distance themselves from the new family; their father, his second wife and their two half-brothers. Like T. J., Kling never went back.

He continued his trade as a sawyer, following the working lumber mills along the Washington and Oregon coasts until his later years. He was known as one of the fastest shingle sawyers in the west. He never lost a finger or hand to the saws. Kling died in 1953 from heart problems. He was seventy-three.

Summer – Fall 1930 – Seattle (Ballard District), Washington

The girls find more than they expected.

Reach out – open the door of faith.

Minnie attended the UW during the summers for around ten years, obtaining her undergraduate and master's degrees. She and the girls stayed with Mackie every summer. The girls slept in the attic, which they accessed by walking through the bedroom of one of the boarders, "Joe" Johansen. He was a family friend of Mackie's from her youth in Grays Harbor. He'd come, like many others of Scandinavian descent, to settle in Seattle's Ballard area and work in the lucrative fishing and boat-building industries.

Mackie's home in Ballard, 2016 NW 56th Street. Courtesy of Puget Sound Regional Archives

On a sunny summer day, Minnie is attending classes, while the girls are at home with Mackie.

Mackie called to the girls. "Gail and Joyce, come and see what Mr. Johansen brought you. It's a special gift from his trip to Texas."

The girls scampered in from playing with marbles on the rug in the front room.

"What is it, Mackie?"

"Well, open the box and see. Be careful now. Open it together." She set the worn cardboard cigar box on the table.

They pulled off the string and lifted the lid.

"Oh, it's so ugly! It has a pointy head. Is it a frog?"

He said it's called a horned toad but it's really a Texas horned lizard."

Joyce reached in the box and petted its back. "It feels crusty like dried mud or leather. Can we keep it in the box?"

"Yes, you can keep it as a pet. You'll have to find something to feed it. Mr. Johansen said it eats a special kind of ant called a harvester ant. I don't think we have those here. He said it also eats beetles, spiders and crickets. Horned toads also like sunny spots, so you can make a little cage for it outside in the yard. We'll find something in the garage tomorrow for you to use."

"Oh, look at him. He's so funny-looking. He looks mean." Gail gently picked it up. "Its stomach is soft like the white bread you buy at the store, grandma Mackie."

"I'll bet you won't eat that again!"

"Yuk." She grimaced. "No, I won't."

Mackie laughed. "Mr. Johansen told me that when it gets scared, it can shoot blood from the corners of its eyes."

Joyce squealed with excitement. "Let's scare him! Maybe he'll do it now." She quickly poked her finger at his throat but barely grazed the side of it. The toad stared at her and blinked.

"No. Let's take him outside and find him some food." Gail gently set the toad back in the box and put the lid on. She clutched it tightly with both hands. Together they darted out the back door and headed for the yard.

Later that night

"You girls can clear the table now. Joyce, you wash dishes tonight. Gail, you dry them and put them on the counter. I'll put them away later."

"Yes, Grandma Mackie," Gail replied. "I need to check on the toad first. We caught five beetles and put them in the box with him so he'd have a good dinner. Come on Joyce, let's see what he's doing." They ran to the front window where the cigar box was set carefully on a carved wooden stool. Gail got there first.

"Oh no, the lid is open and he's gone! Joyce, you didn't put the lid on tight. I knew you wouldn't. How are we going to find him now?" Gail looked around the room in a panic.

Joyce screeched, "I *did* put it on. I even put the string on it. Someone must have opened it. Oh, what are we going to do? Mackie, hurry! The toad is gone. He's somewhere in the house. Help us find him, quick!"

Mackie walked into the living room slowly, wiping her hands on her lavender flower-print apron. She sank into the once-plush chair under her reading lamp. "You girls sit down right over there." She pointed to the sofa.

"I didn't do it. It wasn't my fault." Joyce wailed as tears moistened her eyes. "I put the lid on, I *know* I did. You shouldn't have brought it in the house, Gail. You're older; you should know better." She pouted, perching on the edge of the worn leather seat. She twisted her dark, curly hair with one finger and stared at the empty box, trying to hold back tears.

"I didn't do anything. I asked you to put it away," Gail snapped, sticking her tongue out and glaring at her.

"Hush now. You girls listen. Close your eyes and be still. We will find him. God knows exactly where he is. Just pray now. Know the truth about the toad. Be quiet and feel it, pray about it. Know in your heart he is safe, right here. Hold the right thought and know the truth of this situation."

The clock ticked. The air in the room was thick with expectation. The leftover dinner's now-stale smell of fried chicken, new potatoes and peas wafted in through the kitchen door. Joyce tapped her foot softly against the sofa leg. They all sat. They waited. Time expanded into an eternity of anticipation.

"You can open your eyes now."

The girls opened their eyes. The toad was sitting on the rag rug in front of them. They gasped in delight. "Here he is!"

Joyce grabbed him, thrust him into the box and put the lid on tightly. "There," she declared, "he's safe now."

Gail later recalled this incident in her life story:

> *Mackie said we'd find him. We'd all sit down and know the truth about it. So we did — we prayed and we knew the truth. When we opened our eyes there he was on the rug right in front of us. The magic of knowing the truth was tremendous.*

Late 1920s – Early 1930s — Seattle (Ballard District), Washington

Faith and prayer are more than a few words.

There is a divine plan of goodness for my life.

Mackie joined the Second Church of Christ, Scientist on November 5, 1926, around two months after Joe's death. She'd been drawn to Christian Science because it felt right to her. Through her grief and struggle after her husbands' deaths, she strengthened her faith through prayer, accepted loving help from others and helped them in return. Her beliefs bolstered her. She cared about people and was naturally drawn to be of service.

Her love and empathy for others was palpable. Her eagerness to share her compassion and beliefs led her to become a Christian Science practitioner; to pray with others to resolve and heal life's challenges. People were instinctively drawn to her. She was charismatic and empathic. She never registered with the church as a practitioner because she didn't feel the need to call attention to herself. It wasn't about her. She just did naturally what her love and concern for others led her to do – help them based on her own life experience and beliefs.

Second Church of Christ, Scientist, Seattle, 1937. Courtesy of Puget Sound Regional Archives

Just home from church, Mackie placed a plate of hot, buttered cinnamon rolls by the tea on the table. Anna, her friend from church, pulled out a chair and sat down. She handed Anna a napkin. "I baked these early this morning, and just heated them in the oven. Let's enjoy them."

"Thank you, I'd love to. The sweet, spicy aroma of cinnamon is tantalizing." She smiled, inhaled deeply, and put a roll on her plate.

Mackie laughed. "It's a wonderful fragrance, isn't it? I love to cook. I cook for my boarders and also for Minnie and the girls during the summer."

Anna pulled her chair closer to the table. "It's so good to see you again. It seems like a long time." She looked down at her hands. Her chin trembled. "Mackie, I need someone to talk to. My sister died a month ago. I cared for her before she passed. This is the first time I've been to church since then. I needed time to console myself. We were very close."

"I'm so sorry. I didn't know she was ill."

Anna continued, her voice faltering. "She was doing better until a couple of months ago. Then she got pneumonia; she was already weak and didn't recover. My heart still feels the void of her loss. I walk around the house and stare out the window. I don't know what to do. I can't seem to move past my grief. How did you recover after Joe died? You seem so calm, happy, full of love and joy. How do you do it?"

Mackie pulled up her chair and wiped her hands on a napkin. She gazed out the window at the sunlight striking the fresh green leaves of the huckleberry bush. She turned to Anna. "It was hard." She paused and spoke softly. "Grief is overwhelming. We need to feel our sadness in order to heal. But when we can see it differently, we recognize that our thinking is limited and our loved one still resides in spirit with the same life and vigor, but has merely passed from our sight. Like the shrub outside the window, I may not be able to perceive it through the curtains, but it still lives.

"The key to change is to pray with feeling. Prayer must make an emotional imprint on your mind and heart. Faith and prayer are more than a few words. Put feeling into your prayers and be open to accept the good that God has in store for you. You will recover and know joy again. It requires true belief in action to create what you desire without physical evidence yet in existence."

Anna pulled a tissue from her purse and wiped her eyes. "That makes sense. I know it takes time. I do pray with feeling."

Mackie continued, "Joe's death was the second time I was widowed. My first husband died unexpectedly when I was thirty-three. I was heartbroken. With prayer, God's love and the kind help of friends, I recovered in time. After Joe died, it was different. I was stunned. I thought God had abandoned me. It took me a long time to realize that wasn't true.

"I struggled every day to understand why God had taken my husbands from me. I'd been so happy. Now I was heartbroken again. Joe's death brought back the sorrow I felt when T. J. died. I knew I had to overcome my grief, but I just couldn't find a way. I went to church, read the Bible and *Science and Health.* It soothed me some but I still had tears in my heart. I couldn't close the wound."

She paused and wiped her damp eyes with a tissue. "Just talking about it brings the grief back." She continued, "One evening I sat up late reading. I found an article in the *Christian Science Sentinel* about love. The words seemed to jump off the page right into my broken heart. I'll never forget them. 'When lack appears to be rife, and the world seems cold, even then divine Love sends comfort into the heart.'[15]

"Those words brought me peace. I realized that God still loved me. The love always had been there. I just had to rely on it. It was there for me to take solace in, and to give me comfort. I realized that God is with us despite whatever happens. We need to accept God's love, no matter what. We must know in our hearts that we are loved and taken care of.

We need to love ourselves, too. If we accept and feel unconditional love, we can move forward.

"Here's the amazing part. The *Sentinel* was published the day after Joe died. I was so overcome with grief I didn't even open it until a month later. It was right here on the table just waiting for me."

"That's wonderful. What a blessing for you."

"Yes. I just needed to be able to receive. I took it to heart. It made me stronger and my faith grew. I knew Joe and T. J. were safely in God's care. Now, I hold them in my heart, and God's love holds us all in peace."

"Thank you for sharing. You are such an inspiration to me, Mackie. I feel God's loving presence with me now." Anna sat up straighter. Her face beamed. She picked up her cinnamon roll and took a bite. "Delicious. Thank you."

Mackie Shock, c. 1924

Mackie smiled warmly. "You're welcome, Anna. I'm so happy you feel better. We're all cradled in God's love. We only need to sense it within our hearts."

Mother described Mackie in this way:

Grandmother Mackie had a unique personality. There was a warmth that seemed to protect and comfort you. Everyone loved her. Men were strongly attracted to her, but so were women. I've only known one other person who had this quality.[16]

Mackie remarried again in 1929 to J. B. Kesterson (Mr. Kay). He was sixty-nine, she was fifty-five. He was still a good friend and they saw each other regularly when he came to Seattle. She later said they married for convenience and to quell any rumors about their relationship. He was an original Grays Harbor pioneer in the lumber industry and continued to live there. Around 1932 they stopped seeing each other, as he'd gotten older and couldn't travel any longer. They considered divorce but never formally filed the papers.

Gail told about him in her life story:

> *We just loved that man. Joyce (who later became Trudi) and I could take him on walks every day, lead him to the candy store where he was always good for treats. He was also willing to sit and watch Joyce and me dance – we always took ballet lessons – we dancers were hams and had a perfect audience. . . . Strangely enough they [he and Mackie] never really lived together – he visited from wherever he lived.*

Mackie died of diabetes and bronchial pneumonia in August 1934. She'd struggled with diabetes for four years. It's likely that she, Mr. Kay and Minnie didn't realize its seriousness. She may have attempted to heal herself through Christian Science, but it probably wasn't as important to her as helping others.

1930–1934 – Seattle (Ballard District) and Aberdeen, Washington

Gail's winning essay reveals her sense of humor.

I am a channel for God's creativity and my work comes to good.

In 1934, Gail was a high school junior. *The Aberdeen Daily World* sponsored an essay contest for high school students titled "Why Buy on Grays Harbor." Everyone taking English in high school entered. Twenty-five dollars in prize money was divided among the winners (one from each class: sophomore, junior and senior.) That's the equivalent of approximately $450.00 in 2017 dollars or $150.00 apiece. Gail won the junior class prize.

In the article about the contest, "Why Buy on Grays Harbor," the grammar sounded odd. Shouldn't it be "*in* Grays Harbor?" No. Werner A. Rupp developed this usage when he became the new editor of the

Aberdeen World in June 1908. He wrote a style guide for his editors and reporters. "The harbor" referred to the three main cities around Grays Harbor: Aberdeen, Hoquiam, and Cosmopolis. References to the area were to be "on the harbor," not "in the harbor," which referred to the body of water itself, or something in it. Eventually, this phrase came to refer to all of Grays Harbor County.[17]

Here's Gail's winning essay:

> *I hope you saw that story in "The Aberdeen World" about the sea monster sighted in Puget Sound. If you did, you will be more likely to believe this is a true story.*
>
> *Last Sunday we determined to see that monster. We drove up to Point Defiance Park, Tacoma, with a cargo of foods from soup to nuts. We figured on eating what we wanted and throwing the rest out to bait the monster.*
>
> *Did we see him? I'm telling you, we did!*
>
> *Right in the rocks down the cliff from the park we saw a huge shape just as the story said: four feet, shoulders, a head like a man's. The girls screamed and started to run. I couldn't run, for my knees [had] turned to jelly.*
>
> *Then the monster spoke.*
>
> *"Why didn't you stay home today? You should have driven down to Tokeland. There are some beautiful monsters appearing there today. And one not half bad at Westport."*
>
> *It made me mad.*
>
> *"Who are you and what business is it of yours where we go?"*
>
> *"I'm the old man of the sea. I've a lot to tell you. First build up home resources by using all Harbor-made products possible; fish, oysters, crabs, cheese, milk, butter, eggs, poultry, furniture, roofing, paper, knitted woolens, aprons.*
>
> *"Then buy all other goods from local merchants and keep the middle profits at home, and the home taxes growing.*
>
> *"Employ Grays Harbor professional men – doctors, lawyers, dentists, teachers. Send your children to the local public schools, parochial schools, business college, and junior college. In this way you build up an independent cultural center at home.*

"And last, perhaps most important, pay your bills promptly so these people can keep Grays Harbor-earned money circulating in Grays Harbor, so the bank deposits will grow and back [the] home industries."

"Thanks a lot, and come and see us some time."

"That's another thing. Next Sunday, stay on your own beach. I'll send a choice monster to build up your own tourist trade."

"Thanks, old man."

Then with a splash, he dived.[18]

7 ~ Share the Love

There are more things in heaven and earth, Horatio,
Than are dreamt of in your philosophy.
– Shakespeare

1936 – Aberdeen, Washington

Minnie advances her career.

I embrace my power and manifest my goals.

Minnie received her Master's degree from the UW in 1936. She was a Shakespearean scholar. Her thesis was *Shakespeare's Likeness to Castiglione: An Indication of Probable Indebtedness.* Castiglione (1478–1529) was an Italian courtier, soldier, diplomat, and Renaissance author. He wrote *The Book of the Courtier*, an explanation of court etiquette and morality, which influenced sixteenth-century European court society. Shakespeare (1564–1616) undoubtedly knew of it. Minnie's thesis was that Shakespeare based his plays on Castiglione's ideas, morality, and understanding of human nature. She summarized her thesis this way:

> *What would have been more natural than for Shakespeare, upon arriving in London, or perhaps previously in anticipation of that important event, to possess himself of the courtier's handbook? There he had at once the etiquette book supreme of the court, and a source book of the university wits and court favorites. A country youth with such an equipment, mind and imagination with which to grasp its value, and spirit attuned to recognize his innate kinship with it – such a youth could go far. . . . The very kernel of Shakespeare is to be found in Castiglione's "Courtier." The dramatization of*

Castiglione's ideas and philosophy, – common sense, Platonism, comic-spirit, moral tone, universality, it is all in Shakespeare's plays.[19]

Minnie had arrived in her career. Her positive intention and passion for teaching had paid off. She successfully directed high school senior and one act plays, and coached students for speaking contests. She advised drama groups and served on legislative committees. She taught oral public speaking, advanced dramatics, oral literature and composition in high school, for community groups and at the junior college that opened in the fall of 1930. Her leadership was central to making drama and public speaking prominent in Washington State's public education curriculum.

Summer 1936 – Aberdeen, Washington

Joyce's journal discloses the details.

A journal is like pages from your soul. – Sark

Gail graduated from Weatherwax High in June 1935. She typed Minnie's Master's thesis in spring semester before she graduated. It contained 117 pages, including footnotes. She had to make two carbon copies, correcting them by hand-erasing and retyping. The mechanical typewriters of the 1930s also required hand carriage return and ribbon rewinding. What a project for a high school senior! Gail got her reward, though. In the fall, Minnie sent her to Whitman College in Walla Walla, Washington, not for scholarship (although she received one), but to have a good time and relax.

During her first summer home from college, when Gail was eighteen, she and Joyce wrote diligently in their journals, competing to see who could write the most. Joyce was sixteen and would be a high school junior in the fall. The young women had been writing stories and recording events in their diaries since early childhood. Both Minnie and

Mackie encouraged them. Gail described their childhood writing when she was ten and Joyce was eight:

> *In the winter at 306 E. 3rd Street, Aberdeen, Joyce and I used to sit, on Saturday mornings, in the dining room with our frozen feet propped up on the black metal wood stove (the only heat in a two-story house) and write stories in our notebooks. I wish we had 'em now — I'd like to know whether my style has improved any. Often we wrote "Further Adventures of Penrod and Sam" who were two popular characters in the book of the day. While we wrote, we ate sandwiches of sweet pickles and mayonnaise.*

Their passion for writing later matured into their love of writing short stories, comparing notes and critiquing each other's work in the 1950s. Although neither ever published their stories (as far as I know), they wrote continually.

Joyce was a journalist by nature. She meticulously recorded where they went, who visited and what they ate for dinner. She was outgoing, humorous and fun. Her journal is intact. It is leather-bound, five by eight inches, and it still has the price tag on it – ten cents from Frederick and Nelson (a well-known department store chain based in Seattle from 1891 to 1992).

Joyce was gifted in music, and played in the high school orchestra. She played cello, bass viol, piano and organ. During the summer, she practiced at the high school music department (the Conservatory or "Con") and at home. She named her bass viol "Ermintrude" and her cello "Suzzie." To her, they had the characteristics of people; her good friends. Later in college at the UW, she changed her own name to Trudi after her bass viol.

Gail was involved in her college sorority, Delta Delta Delta ("Tri-Delt"), which focused on character and friendship. She made new friends and enjoyed her freshman year. She'd already met Dick (the man she'd marry) through her sister. He dated Joyce first; but when he and Gail met, they shared a special connection and continued to see each other when they could.

Gail's temperament was unlike her sister's. She was highly sensitive. Her struggle with anxiety influenced how she saw life. Since anxiety was poorly understood, she felt different. Most likely she recorded her feelings, hopes, fears, and plans for returning to college in her journals. She later destroyed them. "Too personal," she said.

Joyce exuberantly wrote about the daily events in their lives, including their interests, friends, and family activities. Below are some of her entries from the summer of 1936.

August 4

Gail and I went to the store at 10 AM on a big spree. Gail had two beautiful phone calls – both wrong numbers but long conversations. For one she said, "You must not want the right person." Mother had a sick headache [migraine] today.

August 6

For once I voluntarily woke – and at 8:30. I had the kitchen all cleaned and had started on the living room by the time Gail stirred. . . . Gail and I went downtown for neck trims, flowers and candy. We dropped by to see Ralph and told him how our radio has been acting up.

We certainly had hard luck with dinner. Poor Mom made two cakes – and the custard tasted like sour pickles to Gail and like oatmeal to me.

I can see why Gail writes so much. It's like a bug – I once got started and now my hand flies so fast I can't stop!

August 14

Up at 8:30. Gave Gail breakfast in bed – pie. No one got any mail this morning. I went to practice – 40 min. cello; 45 min. bass, and rest organ. . . . Tomorrow I shall play Gail a concert. Gail and I had meat balls at 11:30 PM. When I opened the can of Karo tonight, the lid flew off and the Karo spilled all over my face and hair. Now I shall have to wash my hair tomorrow.

August 17

It took me 6-1/2 months to write twenty-seven pages – but with Gail's influence – I've written exactly eighty-two pages in one month and one day.

August 23

Minnie has brought out Gail's old horoscope book. Mine has been missing for years. I was going to analyze my handwriting!

Here's that handwriting analysis: Energy comes in at streaks – you do not control it well enough. . . . Disposition – controlled on the surface, very good natured. Temperament – fairly well balanced. . . . Your friends consider you steady, tactful, useful. For amusement you enjoy music, dancing – parties.

Note: Joyce relished her handwriting analysis while Gail treasured her horoscope from *Fashionable Dress* magazine. It characterized her in this way: "The tenacious Cancer sign has many romantic and exquisite strains making it one of the most charming signs. . . witty, entertaining, sympathetic and protective, but if criticized harshly, or misunderstood, the Cancer-soul becomes grim and antagonistic." It also noted that she would "find it hard to forget little hurts" and "grow more critical as the years advance."[20]

August 24

Juddi's birthday. [Jud, their brother, turned 20]. I got up at 10:00 and Gail had already cleaned the house. [Later] I helped Gail get dinner – she had made some fudge – it was just getting hard. It is sugary but good. Mother came home at 6:15. We had dinner at 6:30. . . . Gail has just stopped [writing]. When we started I was a paragraph ahead of her but now she is about 6 pages ahead of me and we are both writing steadily!

August 30

Jud called about 7:15. [He] said he would be up for "that promised birthday cake." So Mother rushed around and made it and I made the frosting. He arrived and just as we had started to sample it, Gail came home. She was wearing her traditional farmer's outfit and had her hat on straight. She surely looked cute.

Bennie [Ben K. Weatherwax] dropped in about 9:30 to tell mother of a WSC [Washington State College] opening. The woman who taught drama has left. But the opening is for THIS year. Benny left very shortly after.

Gail seemed to have a very good time [at the party]. However – one of the girls told her that Dick is not going back to school. I hope she will see him anyhow. It is hard to tell how much she loves him – for her sake I hope nothing happens to keep them from seeing each other.

Sept. 8

SCHOOL's ON. Gail and I went to town. Teacher's Institute; Mother goes all day. Continue music sorting job at Con.

I went home – Gail was all packed and had her room all cleaned. Which I certainly appreciate! Mother came home at 3. . . . Gail left presents on our dresser – two gorgeous powder puffs apiece. Gail called Mae at 3:30 and then we walked downtown. I stopped at the Broadway for a "Confessions" magazine for Gail to read on the train [to return to college]. . . . Just as Gail boarded the train, Juddie presented her with a cute little box wrapped in red and white – some "Tweedie's" toilet water.

[illegible] has brought out Gail's old horoscope book [illegible] Mine has been missing for years. Are we having fun! That's right!! I was going to analyze my handwriting! (I hope no one reads this!)

Well – seven pages are enough! Besides the day is over! Tomorrow I think I shall analyze my handwriting!

Page from Joyce's Journal August 1936

Joyce's journal entry says:

> *Minnie has brought out Gail's old horoscope book. Mine has been missing for years. Are we having fun! That's right!!! I was going to analyze my handwriting (I hope no one reads this!)*
>
> *Well - seven pages are enough! Besides, the day is over. Tomorrow I think I shall analyze my "handiwork."*

1937–1938 – Aberdeen and Seattle, Washington

Minnie attains another goal.

Greater things are coming to you – just continue your thoughts and actions. It's all ahead.

Minnie's brief year-end journal entry revealed an exciting new career development.

> *December 31, 1937 – moved to Seattle – job at Roosevelt High School – Elvena's job recommendation.*

She started teaching at Roosevelt High School on January 3, 1938. It's located around a mile north of the UW. It is still known for having one of the best high school theatre departments on the West Coast.

At Roosevelt, Minnie's teaching roles in drama and English continued. She also pursued her Ph.D. degree at the UW. She ultimately decided not to complete her dissertation. She was finally ready to relax. She said she'd rather go fishing on Orcas Island with her friend, housemate, and former student, Betty Hopper.

Minnie always lived in the University or Roosevelt Districts, part of the "North End" of Seattle. After a few years, she lived in the house that Joe and Mackie had purchased on NE 72nd Street, just off Roosevelt Way NE; a beautiful craftsman home that was razed in the late '60s to build an apartment building. It is the house I recall from childhood.

Minnie's home, 916 NE 72nd Street, Seattle. Courtesy of Puget Sound Regional Archives

Gail did not return to Whitman for her junior year, but attended business college in Aberdeen, and then moved with Minnie to Seattle. Once in Seattle, she and Dick were able to see each other regularly again.

Joyce stayed with friends in Aberdeen so she could graduate from Weatherwax High in June 1938. She then moved to Seattle to attend the UW.

1940s – Seattle, Washington

The happy couple

In love all life is given, in love all things move. – Edgar Cayce

Gail and Dick were married in a quiet ceremony at the University Unitarian Church on 35th Avenue N.E. in Seattle, on September 7, 1940. During World War II, weddings were often simple due to rationing of basic supplies and imminent deployment. Fortunately, Dick was already supporting the war effort. He worked at the Bremerton Naval Shipyard in engineering as a *Progressman*, reviewing ship installation drawings to identify maintenance items.

September 7, 1940, 10:00 AM – Seattle, Washington

Dick and Gail nervously walked up to the large, carved church doors. "Do you think anyone is here yet?" Gail asked.

Just then, Reverend Alexander Winston flung the door open. "Good morning. Are you ready for the ceremony?" He gave them a welcoming smile and ushered them inside.

Dick laughed. "We were wondering if you were here yet. We're ready, reverend. We're excited too."

"Wonderful. I love to perform weddings. Come in and we'll get set up."

Gail wore her "soldier-blue" dress. The faint peppery-spice scent of her pink Cecil Brunner sweetheart-rose corsage wafted around her. She gave the minister her biggest smile. "We are ready." She looked around at the church interior. The lighting was soft, the altar flowers beautiful. Their witnesses, Jud and a family friend, Mrs. Harry Rasmussen, walked in the door behind her.

Minnie followed them. "This is the day!" she announced as she entered the church door. "I'm so happy for you both."

A few guests entered and were ushered to their seats. Reverend Winston stood in front of the group solemnly. The organ music began the short ceremony and they repeated their vows. Reverend Winston concluded, "Inasmuch as you have sealed your vows before the group gathered here, by giving these rings, and have consented to live together in the state of marriage, I pronounce you husband and wife." Dick looked at Gail and smiled.

"You may kiss the bride."

Dick looked down at her. She was so petite, innocent, and sweet. She looked lovely. Her eyes caught his, and she smiled as she looked into them. *He's the one. I felt something special about him the day we met.* She felt her heart expand with love; it shone through her eyes. He leaned down, tenderly touched her face and opened his lips slightly. He looked into her eyes, wide with expectation. His lips touched hers gently. She stood on her tiptoes, reaching up to his six-foot-plus frame, pressing her lips into his. He put his arms around her and held her tightly as their lips met. Their love expanded and poured into each other with the tenderness of their kiss. Then he released her. She looked up at him, her eyes full of love.

Dick smiled and turned to the minister. Everyone cheered as they walked down the aisle. Jud laughed, reached out and slapped Dick on the back as he passed. "Congratulations! Welcome to the family."

Minnie's journal entry revealed her happiness:

Sept. 7, 1940 – Gail and Dick married at University Unitarian Church. Breakfast after at Betty Jenks. Lovely wedding. Very happy tone. Gail beautiful. Dick and Jud handsome.

Dick and Gail's wedding day 9/7/1940

8 ~ Embrace the Challenge of Change

In relationships, we confront both what is easy and difficult to accept about our nature. – Angeles Arrien

1940s – Bremerton and Seattle, Washington

First thoughts have tremendous energy. It is the way the mind first flashes on something. – Natalie Goldberg

Gail was gone and Minnie missed her. Her brief journal entry the day after Gail and Dick's wedding hinted at her feelings:

Sept 8, 1940 – First day without Gail.

Now they visited and corresponded. They lived across Puget Sound from each other; a ferry ride of less than an hour (the Navy Yard Route) from Seattle to Bremerton, where Dick and Gail had settled in the South Court Apartments. When the couple traveled across the Sound at night, they often took the ferry called *Kalakala,* which operated from 1935 to 1967. She was known for her streamlined superstructure. Her art deco styling and luxury included an evening dance band. Since Dick had played the clarinet in the UW orchestra and loved music, it was a perfect venue for their evening.

Minnie wrote to Gail in the early 1940s, commenting on her life with her typical zany humor:

Sunday

Hello Stinky. Why don't you write? I almost came over on the seven o'clock ferry this morn, the cause being that Robin [Jud's wife – he was

deployed in Europe] got me up at six to have breakfast with her on account [of] she feels so damn sorry for herself getting up alone on Sunday. The reason I didn't come, which was a pity seeing there was a ride for me as far as Marion Street, was because I discovered we didn't have enough cash between us and we weren't among friends at breakfast. Besides, I don't like to come without bringing my calories with me, rationing being what it is and the high cost of living.

In my futile, impractical way, I have been refraining from using Jud's typer [typewriter] so it would be good when he comes home from the goddam wars. Now I discover it was the wrong thing to do. The obscene thing has corroded all to hell — so it has no nice shiny finish and the keys stick — so for each letter I have to half stand, gather for a spring and madly fling all my two-hundred-plus-poundage right at the spot. Juddy is going to berate me soundly – which is a pity, for I'd be a gentle, sweet old lady if I didn't live such a hard life.

I'm writing a story. Must get at it. Love to Dick and the Siamese kitty. Must see them and you soon. Can you come over? What the hell for your imminent birthday?

Minnie Mooneye

Minnie and Tryout Theatre – Seattle, Washington

They always just called it "Tryout." – Jorj Savage (George Savage, Jr.), playwright

Minnie was one of the founding members of Tryout Theatre in Seattle. George M. Savage, a UW Associate Professor of English, and a playwright, met with twenty-five other theater professionals in May 1943, to discuss the possibility of a post-war theatre for playwrights. They moved forward quickly, forming a non-profit organization and charging themselves $10 apiece for dues. The first play, *Blue Alert*, a wartime comedy by Zoe Schiller and George Savage, opened in August 1943.

Tryout was a venue for playwrights to see their work in production (and make appropriate changes) before it was formally

Minnie Moore McDowell, c. 1946

produced elsewhere. This novel concept allowed the playwright to take part in the revision process. In the first year, the theatre produced seven plays, and 105 different people appeared in roles in Tryout productions.[21] Tryout was active in Seattle through the late 1940s.

There was no upstaging in this group. Minnie's role included public relations, various positions on the executive board, reading and evaluating plays, acting and directing. She wrote several articles about Tryout, which were published in various theatre publications.[22]

Her enthusiasm and passion for the theatre beamed through every article. About the theatre's founding, she said:

> Tryout Theater, in Seattle, Washington, which gave its first public performance August 3, 1943, is a little theatre founded on a big idea. Since that August date, Tryout theatre has put on five plays, all from manuscript, plays which have not been published or produced in their present form in any other theatre. The purpose of the theatre is to promote the writing of more and better plays and to give practical aid to the playwright by putting his play to the test before an audience.[23]

Her solid belief in experimental theatre as an art form persuades us still:

> As we approach the close of our first year we are amazed that we can keep going. Sometimes we wonder where the next play is coming from, but there has always been one when we were ready for it. We know a play isn't written, but grows as the larch, the beech, and the oak, sometimes slowly, with pruning, grafting, and

cultivation. It is the aim of the Tryout Theatre to give the playwright a chance for surgery and conservation.[24]

December 1943 – Bremerton, Washington

Dick and Gail start their family.

Remember your soul is reborn many times into the unknown darkness. It triumphs every time.

A tiny, underweight baby gasped for air and cried. The doctor untangled the umbilical cord from around her neck. *This baby came too early and is underweight. We'll be lucky if we can keep her alive.* He handed the tiny baby to the nurse. "Congratulations, Mrs. Stradling. It's a girl."

I was that baby. Born three weeks early, I weighed four pounds, seven ounces, and remained in the hospital for ten days. Once home, I cried constantly and endured repeated projectile vomiting. Breastfeeding was out of fashion. Formula was scientific, and the pediatrician wrote numerous scripts. Three of them were: homogenized milk and Karo syrup; evaporated milk, sugar and water; and goat's milk with water. Sound tasty and nutritious? It didn't to me either.

Gail was exhausted from her new routine of formulas, feedings, and vomiting. "Dick, could you take her tonight? I have to get some sleep. She frustrates me so. She's a difficult baby to care for and love. She cries all the time and throws up on everything, even me and the floor. I need some rest. She's on the four-hour feeding schedule. The doctor said to put her in her crib and let her cry if you have to."

"Well, okay I guess. I'll hold her for a while, and see if she throws up before I put her down."

She handed him the baby. "Please don't wake me; I need sleep badly." She turned, went into the bedroom, and shut the door.

He took the little girl and sank into the old wooden rocking chair in the living room, propping her into the curve of his arm. "Now, now, Julius, just relax. Everything's going to be all right. I'll hold you until you fall asleep." *I wish you'd been a boy; you probably wouldn't have been so fussy. I would have named you Julius, so that's what I call you now.*

He rocked her gently. The last formula didn't agree with her either. She twisted back and forth, choked violently and threw up on her blanket and shirt.

"Oh my God, here we go again."

He held her to his chest gently, and patted her back. "Julius, are you okay?" he whispered. He sighed, cleaned her up, changed her diaper and shirt, and wrapped her in a clean blanket. "I'll put you in your crib. It's still a couple of hours before feeding time. Here you go." He put her down gently, covered her with another blanket, switched off the light and pulled the door shut firmly behind him.

I twist and turn again. My stomach aches. I'm alone. There is no one to hold me. No warmth or comfort. Pain engulfs my abdomen, making me tremble and squirm. I'm hungry and cold. I shriek. Why doesn't someone hear me? I cry harder. A spasm of pain shoots through my stomach again. My whole body convulses. The room is dark. I kick my blanket off, and writhe in pain. No one comes for me. I cry into the darkness until I fall asleep hungry and exhausted.

Dad wanted a boy. Mom wasn't ready for children. She'd been the eldest of the girls and Minnie's helper for years. She wasn't prepared for a sickly, fussy baby. She hadn't bonded with her baby due to the 1940s medical "hands off" policy, which prevented parents from handling preemies to protect them from infection. The scientific four-hour feeding schedule was inappropriate for a preemie and the nutrient-deficient formulas had little nourishment. My life began as a challenge.

1951 – Bellingham, Washington

Gail becomes pregnant again.

It is not so much overcoming as it is accepting and letting go.

After my feeding difficulties were resolved, Dick and Gail's lives flowed with a fresh rhythm. They enjoyed visiting friends, playing cards and badminton. Dick continued working at the Navy Yard while he studied for the Washington State architect's license exam. They bought property in Bothell, part of the Seattle metro area just north of the city, where they remodeled a small house, experimented with organic gardening, raised farm animals and planned a truck farm to sell their blueberries commercially. In the late 1940s, they moved to Bellingham where Dick started his architecture business.

After they became established in Bellingham, and Dad's business grew, they wanted to expand their family. By then I was almost eight. Gail had worried that she'd never be able to get pregnant again. Finally she did, and gave birth to another baby girl, Stephanie Gail. She was thrilled. Although Gail had been home from the hospital for almost three weeks, her baby was still there. She visited Stephanie every day, hoping she'd soon be strong enough to come home.

Up early this morning, she cleaned the kitchen. She felt uneasy, anxious. *I just can't sit down today. I have to keep busy. It's too early to visit Stephanie Gail. I wonder what I can do next. I guess I'll sweep and mop; it will keep me busy.*

The phone rang and she picked up the receiver. "Hello."

"Good morning, Mrs. Stradling. This is Dr. Neils at St. Joseph's Hospital. I'm sorry to call you so early in the morning. I have bad news. Your infant daughter didn't make it through the night. As you know, she had pneumonia and atelectasis – a partial collapse of a lung. Her death was probably due to aspiration of vomitus. We did everything we could for her. I am so sorry. I regret giving this kind of news to anyone, especially to you and Dick. I know you've been worried. We tried hard to save her. I'm very sorry."

Gail's breath caught sharply in her throat. She felt her stomach tighten and her heart race. "No!" She gasped. "My . . . my . . . baby," she stammered. "I can't believe it. Not my Stephanie Gail. She was going to get better. I . . . can't talk now." Sobs caught in her throat. She hung up the phone. She sank down numbly on the yellow vinyl kitchen chair and buried her head in her hands. She wailed, "No, no, no."

She moaned, lay her head on the kitchen table, sobbing uncontrollably. She struggled to breathe. "I can't take any more," she wailed through her sobs, "I'll never get over this. I'll never have another baby." She wiped her face on her sleeve and began sobbing again, her sobs bursting out in choking gasps. *I have to call Dick.* But she couldn't force her body up off the chair or reach for the phone. She cradled her head in her hands on the table again, sobbing a pool of warm, wet tears on the cold, shiny surface.

Stephanie Gail died at three weeks. I never saw her. I was never told anything about her birth or death. Her birth certificate was kept in the Chinese secretary for years. The entire experience was never mentioned again.

c. 1952 – St. Joseph's Hospital, Bellingham, Washington

The point of power is always in the present moment. – Louise Hay

Within a few months after her baby died, Gail became very ill, and her doctor sent her to St. Joseph's Hospital to recover. In the early morning, she lay motionless in the hospital bed.

"Good morning, Mrs. Stradling. How are you feeling today?"

Her eyelids flickered as she turned slowly toward the sound of the doctor's voice. She moaned, "Ummm . . . not so good."

"I'm sorry to hear that. I'll send the nurse right in. We don't know for sure what your problem is. We're still studying your symptoms and the tests. I'm calling in a specialist. You could have stomach or colon cancer, or possibly Hirschsprung's disease. Based on your history, you've had stomach and intestinal problems all your life. They have worsened significantly. We may need to operate. You rest now. We're going to put you on more penicillin, and I'll try another regimen if that isn't effective."

Gail turned her head, opened her eyes and moaned softly. "Can't you just take away the pain, doctor?"

"I'll have the nurse increase your dosage. She'll check on you in fifteen minutes."

She tried to turn to her side, squeezing her eyes shut to hold back tears. "Oh please God," she whispered, "give me the courage and strength to deal with this illness." She took a deep breath to relax, and lapsed into a semi-awake state, still conscious of the pain in her lower body.

She remained in the hospital for several weeks. I was sent to live with my paternal grandparents in their double-wide trailer in Bremerton. I recall squeezing into the cramped breakfast nook for meals, and my grandfather relishing huge salads from their garden. "Rabbit food," he called it.

Nothing was ever mentioned about Mother's illness or the resolution. When I returned home, life proceeded as if nothing had happened. Gail recovered and was much better for the next half dozen years. Then she underwent a long series of abdominal surgeries from my junior high years through early college, resulting in a permanent colostomy bag. Years later, her doctor told her she should never have had surgery. Neither my siblings nor I recall – or perhaps we never knew – her diagnosis.

After returning home from her first hospital stay, Gail wrote her sister, Trudi:

Thursday March 13, 1952

Well, dear girl,

I have just come from the Drs. and been pronounced 100 percent cured. However I am not the same percent perfect. If you thunk I looked a wee bit bald when we visited your establishment and tasted of the fine Chinese fare, you should see me now! My god, more than half my hair is gone, and last night I had to make myself a hat which will remain on my head 24 hours a day 'till I once again have a crowning glory. Unfortunately 'tis still falling out by the bucket load.

9 ~ Reframe Stressful Situations

Your loved ones are never out of reach – not now or ever – for souls are constantly in communication with each other.
– Doreen Virtue

April 1949 – Seattle, Washington

Minnie embraces another change.

There is no death, only a change of worlds. – Chief Seattle

Minnie continued her career at Roosevelt High. If you could eavesdrop on Minnie's house at 916 NE 72nd Street, you'd sense a hub of energy and creativity; hear loud talking and laugher, script-reading, directing, cross-talk, comments, and critique. Minnie taught directing in her home. She stimulated her students with intellectual passion and genuine creativity. Her presence alone accelerated learning.

Everything about Minnie was big – her stature, energy, enthusiasm, happiness, laughter and wacky sense of humor. She was "always young" like the name of the skin cream she wore, Sem-Pray Jo-Ve-Nay. She loved clothes. Her daily costumes were capes, suits, bright colors, flamboyant floral patterns. She announced, "It's people like me who set the styles." She did. Her charisma expanded the cosmos. Even her signature had her characteristic flair.

Minnie woke early on Wednesday morning, April 6th. *Oh boy, I feel rough today. Must be old age.* She laughed to herself as she opened the curtains slightly. It was a beautiful April morning, warmer than usual for April.

It's going to be warm today. I'd better dress in layers. She opened the bedroom window a crack. It felt like spring. She heard birds singing in the fruit trees out back. *What a fabulous day. I'd better get going. I have a lot to do.*

She pulled on her robe and slippers and made her way to the kitchen. Then she turned back toward the bedroom. *I guess I'll just bathe and dress now. Then I'm sure to be ready when Edna picks me up.*

She performed her daily routine. She bathed, brushed her teeth, pulled her hair back and combed it. She'd had it trimmed so it was shorter now, easier to do. *That's good. I can get out of here faster in the morning.* She dressed, selecting her dark blue dress with a V neckline and a strand of pearls. She pulled out a bright, pink-and-blue flower-patterned jacket to wear when she left the house.

She walked into the kitchen. "Juxie!" she exclaimed. "You silly cat. I almost forgot you this morning. Why didn't you come and wake me? You're so independent. I guess you decided to wait today, didn't you?"

Juxie looked up at her and meowed loudly.

She bent down, and ran her hand across her black cat's back. Juxie raised her back and the slightest stub of a tail. "Juxie, you're a Manx, you don't have a tail I can pet." She laughed. Juxie stretched up to meet her, rubbing her head against Minnie's hand and purring. She licked Minnie's finger.

"Oh, I bet you're hungry and want to go out. Come on, now. Let's get some breakfast."

Minnie with Juxie, 1940s

She put cat food in Juxie's dish and opened the back door. "Here you go." She set the dish down on the small wooden porch. The narrow stairway descended into the lush backyard. She attached a long chain to Juxie's collar.

"You can be outside today. It's a nice day and it will be warm, too. We don't want you to get hit by a car now, do we? Maybe you can catch a mouse. Look in the tall grass over there under the little apple tree." She waved her hand toward the back fence. She petted Juxie again, and shut the door.

Well, let's see. I'm going to have toast for breakfast; I'll eat lightly today. My stomach doesn't feel so good; I feel like I have heartburn or something. She patted her chest. *It's coming up into my chest too. Toast will be just enough. I'd better put on the teakettle. Hot tea will refresh me.*

She filled the teakettle with water, turned on the back burner and put it on the stove. The toast popped up, so she took it out, put it on the plate, buttered it lightly and set it on the table at her usual place. *I don't need a lot this morning,* she thought. *Even my back, arm and jaw feel sensitive today. My chest feels tight, too. Oh well, I'll get better as the day goes on. At least I haven't had a migraine lately. That's a relief.*

The teakettle started to whistle. She put a pink flowered napkin by her plate, and glanced at the wooden clock on the east wall. *It's almost 7:00 AM now. I'd better be ready soon. Edna is always on time to pick me up. I'll get my papers together after I pour my tea.*

She turned from the table and took a couple of steps. Suddenly she felt lightheaded. She reached back, grabbed the table edge and paused. She let go, and took a few more uncertain steps. *Oh dear, what's happening? I feel like my legs are giving way. I'm dizzy. I'm going to fall!* She started to black out as a sharp, blinding pain suddenly drove through her chest, left arm and back. She dropped heavily to the floor gasping. Her 200 pounds lay motionless on the kitchen floor as the teakettle whistled relentlessly. She barely heard it. She couldn't move or breathe. Excruciating pain intensified through her body, rendering her paralyzed. She lost consciousness. Darkness enveloped her.

Almost as suddenly, she sensed she was being lifted up, floating on the ceiling, looking down at her body. She realized she'd left it. She had died. She sensed being tugged, pulled, lifted higher into emptiness, moving swiftly through a dark tunnel, higher and farther away from the room, the house, the atmosphere of Earth. She felt lighter, free. Instantly, her energy blended into blissful, golden light. She felt deep peace, oneness with all, joy, radiance and unconditional love. She had transcended.

The phone rang in the kitchen of the little house in Bothell. Gail set down her coffee and picked up the receiver. "Hello."

"Good morning. Is this Mrs. Stradling?"

"Yes it is. Who's this?"

"This is Dr. Wilson. Are you Minnie McDowell's daughter?"

"Yes. Why?" She recognized the familiar, anxious flutter in her chest. Her stomach tightened instantly.

"Mrs. Stradling, I have sad news. Mrs. McDowell died this morning. She had a heart attack at her home."

"What?" Her mind felt numb. She could scarcely breathe. "What . . . what did you say?" she suddenly felt weak, lightheaded. She grasped the threadbare arm of the pale blue couch and gingerly lowered herself onto it.

"Yes, Mrs. Stradling, I am so sorry to tell you this. Your mother died around 7:00 AM this morning from a massive heart attack. She was found on the floor of her kitchen by a friend."

"What? No, I don't believe it. I saw her just a couple of days ago. She came to dinner. She was fine. There was nothing wrong with her. It can't be true."

"I'm so sorry. It's likely she had hypertensive heart disease for a long time, and there were no symptoms. You'll need to provide the information for the death certificate."

Gail slowly hung up the phone. She felt disoriented, frozen. She couldn't think. Her whole body was numb. She stared out the window vacantly. *Momma, where are you? You can't be gone just like that.* Her heart felt empty. Her body was heavy. *Momma, how could you? How could you be gone? I can't imagine living without you.*

"Oh, Momma," she wailed. She crumpled into the corner of the couch and started to cry. "Where are you? I have to see you again. I don't believe it." She buried her head in the blue-and-white striped pillows and sobbed. Finally she lifted her head; looked around the modest room of the little house. *I don't want to be here. There's no reason to live now.*

She got up, blew her nose, walked to the window. The damp green trees across the small clearing caught a ray of sunshine. She squeezed her hand into a fist and slammed it against the wall. *Not without you, Momma.* She threw herself on the couch again and started sobbing.

Why? Why? She could scarcely form the words in her mind. She lifted her wet face from the pillow and whispered, "Momma, Momma, where are you?" Her eyes were bloodshot and swollen. She could barely see the room through her tears. She lay her head back on the pillow, alternately sobbing and choking on her words, "Oh, no, Momma. Gone? No!"

She lay there for a long time. Finally, she forced her thin frame to a sitting position. She felt disoriented. Her hands trembled as she picked up the phone to call Dick. *What will I do without Momma? I loved her so much. The greatest momma in the world.*

She didn't mention Minnie's name for ten years. She later recalled:

> *I was dumbfounded when Minnie died, because she had always been the same – doing her theatre stuff, teaching at her house, full of fun, enthusiasm, laughter, new projects, new ideas . . . and she was so young, only fifty-four. It was such a shock, I couldn't get over it. And I loved her so much. She wasn't much of a mother but she was a great person. You couldn't help but love her. And I did – with all my heart.*

Summer 1949 – Seattle (Bothell area), Washington

Dick and Gail launch their financial independence.

You have help. Miracles are happening every day; you just don't recognize them. Allow your good to unfold.

Minnie died in April 1949. Dick and Gail were still remodeling their house in Bothell, working on their property and preparing to start a small truck farm.

Dick leaned his worn shovel against the house and wiped his forehead with the back of his hand. "It's time for a beer. We've worked hard today, digging in both the basement and the garden." He stepped inside the small house, got out two Rainier beers and opened them. "Here you go, dear. Good work today." He handed one to Gail and grinned. “I’m glad your father has stock in Rainier. Hopefully we’ll help it go up.” He laughed as he took a sip.

They sat in their red and blue lawn chairs in front of the little house at 2539 NE 96th Street in Bothell. They had purchased it in September 1946. Originally a large chicken coop that had morphed into a small home, Dick had remodeled it using his architectural expertise. A large organic vegetable garden graced the clearing in the trees. A small shed and fenced area stood adjacent to it. On the other side of the house, another plot was partially dug up, with piles of pungent-smelling dirt and brush alongside.

Stradling home, 2539 NE 96th St.,
Seattle (Bothell), 1947
Courtesy of Puget Sound Regional Archives

Gail perused the property, overseeing every detail. “Do you think if we plant blueberries like we planned, we can sell enough at the Pike Place Market to make a profit? We’re pretty independent already. We have Homer, our pig, the chickens and our vegetable garden. And we’ve got all those books on organic gardening and how to make a profit on a truck farm.”

“I don’t know. I’ve been thinking about making money too. I want to be permanently independent. I don’t know if we can do that here. I think I should start my own business. I have my Washington State architecture license now. I’d like to get serious about starting an architecture practice. Here in Seattle there’s a lot of competition. I think it would be smart to move to a smaller town.”

“Really? You’re not thinking of moving back to Bremerton, are you?”

Dick put down his beer and laughed. “Oh, no, I’m thinking about Bellingham. It’s about ninety miles north of here. We could easily see our families. It’s only around a three hour drive on Highway 99. What do you think?”

Gail looked across at him dubiously, twisting the beer bottle in her hands. “Well, we’ve done a lot of work on this place with all our gardening, remodeling, and preparation to start a truck farm. I’d hate to leave it now." She sighed, and surveyed their work in progress again. "But, if that's what you want to do, I guess we could give it a try. It would be a great adventure."

"We could start fresh in a different town, with new opportunities. It would be easier to make friends in a smaller town."

"I guess you're right. Well, okay, let's do it."

Dad moved to Bellingham in 1949; the family followed in 1950. He started his architecture business on Commercial Street across from the Bellingham Hotel, with his business partner, Doryanne Miller. We rented a house at 2309 "G" Street; an older two-story home, still standing, and well kept. We lived in four rentals around town before Dad's business was successful enough for him to buy property in the Edgemoor area and build his showcase home in the late 1950s.

1950s–1960s – Bellingham, Washington

Family dysfunction reigns.

Nothing terrible has ever happened except in our thinking. . . . The worst that can happen to you is your uninvestigated belief system. – Byron Katie

Gail's health improved after Stephanie Gail's death and her mysterious illness. She was able to get pregnant again. My sister, Starr, was born in 1953, and my brother, Geoff, in 1955.

When Starr was born, I was ten. I couldn't grasp the extraordinary attention she received. I'd been protected from all of Gail's trauma, illness and losing the baby. I instantly became jealous. I felt abandoned by parents I'd never felt close to. I withdrew, finding comfort with imaginary friends, books, and nature. At that time, we lived in a woodsy, developing area on Alabama Hill. I enjoyed exploring the woods. I created make-believe herbal concoctions and studied wildlife. I launched my life-long habits: gardening, herbal lore, birdwatching and fascination with the natural world. Nature became my teacher.

After around a year and a half, we moved back into town and lived on 15th Street (and later on 13th Street) on Bellingham's south side, the Fairhaven district, where Dad eventually built the family home. After

Geoff was born, the household dynamic quickly transformed into two distinct families. I became Mother's helper, as Gail had been to Minnie.

Gail continued to struggle with the anxiety she'd experienced as a teen. She developed agoraphobia and was often too anxious to leave the house. I was twelve when she insisted I take the bus downtown to buy her favorite cosmetics, Pond's Cold Cream and Revlon Fire & Ice lipstick. I was terrified. Like her, I suffered from anxiety and had zero sense of direction. She may not have realized it, or perhaps she wanted me to do what she could not.

We always called our parents by their first names. We were treated as miniature adults. There was no affection or pampering in our family – or even a sense of family. Gail re-created the style of parenting and family she'd known as a child after Minnie and Kling's divorce, with a working mother and absent father.

During my junior high years, my weekends typically revolved around her demands that I help her with housework. With two small children, she needed help. She acted as if my sole purpose was to serve her needs without question. I learned to have no healthy emotional boundaries, not to stand up for myself or feel valued for being me. Her indifferent approach and abrupt communication style probably resulted from her stress and anxiety. I didn't understand that of course; I only knew that it triggered my sensitive emotions.

Saturday morning, 9:00 AM

Gail pushed open my bedroom door. I was expecting her. I was dressed in my old clothes, lounging on my bed, arranging my bed doll's tiered chartreuse skirt. I already had a sense of style, décor and beauty like both Gail and Minnie. Bright colors and simple, cheerful surroundings lifted my spirits.

She brusquely outlined the day's work. "Okay, it's Saturday again – time to clean house and do laundry. I want you to vacuum, dust, and gather the laundry from the kids' bedroom so I can do it. Be sure to put their toys away under the table in the playroom before you vacuum. When you're done with that, you can water the house plants. If I get a load of laundry done by then, you can hang it on the clothesline.

"Tonight you'll have your first cooking lesson. I want you to learn how to cook dinner in case I need your help. We'll have Swiss steak and scalloped potatoes. Later, you can gather some lettuce and other vegetables from the garden for a salad. Let's get started. It shouldn't take you long."

I got up off my bed. I hung my head as I walked into the hall. I dragged the old Hoover out of the hall closet, plugged it in and flipped the switch. It roared into action. I choked back a sob as tears formed in the corners of my eyes. *Saturday again. I hate this day. Why do I have to do this? What does she do anyway? The kids don't even have to pick up their own toys. I do it for them.*

I ran the vacuum quickly around the living room and turned it off. Toys were scattered all over the play room (the dining room makeover). I grabbed them up in bunches, threw them into the cardboard boxes that doubled as toy boxes and shoved them under the wooden door which was propped up on concrete blocks – Dad's DIY play table. I grabbed the vacuum again and ran it over the worn carpet. *Maybe I can get this done before she realizes it and get out of here. Oh, I forgot – dusting is next. I'd better do it now – she'll inspect my work.*

I dragged the vacuum back to the closet and shoved it in. I grabbed a dust cloth and headed for the Chinese secretary in the living room. This beautiful antique had been in Minnie's house when I was a child. She'd kept marbles, cards and a few plastic cars in the bottom drawer for me when we visited. I hated it now. It featured a curved top, carved and elaborately painted black-and-white, crackle-finish doors displaying paintings of beautiful Chinese women. The doors opened to shelves and mail slots inside. Below, the carved drawers displayed intricate metal pulls. Ornately-fashioned legs and stretcher bars provided its support. Every tiny part collected dust. I could never get it clean. *Why try?* I ran the dust cloth over it quickly.

I finished dusting. Back in the kitchen, I stepped out onto the porch, shook the cloth and put it away. I filled the watering can and dumped water on her neat rows of potted plants, arranged on the breakfast nook's wide, white windowsills.

"Okay, I'm done now." It seemed like dinnertime already. *Oh no, I have to cook tonight.*

"Let's check your work." She walked through the living room. "It doesn't look like you dusted the table; the magazines haven't been stacked." She ran her finger along the ledge of the secretary. "This could use a better job. I'll check the kids' room next." She walked to the back of the house, and looked around.

"You didn't do anything in here. What's the matter with you, anyway? Finish the front room, pick up the laundry, do the kids' room, finish dusting, and you'll be done."

I hung my head. *I'm never good enough. She's never happy with me. I can't do anything right.* I walked slowly back to the living room, avoiding her gaze in the hall. I turned my head so she wouldn't see the tears in my eyes. I finished the chores. I was done at last. I grabbed my frayed jacket from the tiny hall closet and slipped silently out the back door.

I sought my solace alone. I walked through the alleys of the surrounding neighborhood, enjoying the abundance of flower and vegetable gardens that spilled out over broken fences onto the dirt and gravel. Squash, Shasta daisies and nasturtiums bloomed yellow, white and orange, surrounding garbage cans, and spreading across the rusted fenders of old junkers. I still loved plants from my childhood in the woods. Their natural beauty calmed my mind as I wiped my tears.

Walking comforted me. I prayed: *The Lord is my shepherd. . . .* The hopeful psalm soothed me. By the time forty-five minutes had flown by, I returned home, having raised my courage to face more criticism, rejection, and abandonment. My release was writing in my journal – a habit that served me well over my lifetime.

I was introverted, quiet, and studious. I enjoyed being alone. I read voraciously, and explored art with watercolors and drawing. With two creative parents, our cabinet drawers were stocked with drawing paper, paints and colored pencils. Dick regularly brought home samples of building materials that hopeful contractors had enticed him with – "bribes" he affectionately called them. I built things with them. Gail played with paper dolls as a child, so I made those too. I amused myself; a blessing that allowed me to cultivate my innate talents.

Gail's intestinal problems flared up again, dramatically. Through the next eight to ten years, she survived nine major surgeries and twelve minor ones. She was always in the hospital or recovering. Lying in bed at night, I heard her crying in pain. I feared she would die. I curled up in my bed, burying my head under blankets and pillows, but I couldn't shut out the sound of her sobs.

Her illness was never discussed. I struggled to understand this deeply disturbing family secret. Close family friends knew, of course. They stopped by while she was in the hospital or home recuperating, bearing a huge variety of casseroles that all tasted the same. Mums from her hospital stays were a fixture on the kitchen table and the back porch for years.

As my siblings matured, Dad's business became successful. We were finally middle class. Dick and Gail had relaxed from their stressors: poverty, personal loss, illness, trauma and anxiety. But the family remained dysfunctional. We were all "abandoned" children, not from the basic comforts of life, but from love, attention, importance. The abandoned child learns to become invisible to survive and please the parental giants of his/her world. We did. I was rarely allowed to spend the night at a girlfriend's house, attend a birthday party, or socialize much with friends outside of school. Dad always said, "You might be needed at home." He often reminded me that I was "only a small cog in a big wheel."

Naturally a seeker, I explored philosophy, psychology, art, religion. I taught myself self-hypnosis and meditation at thirteen – my tactic to find peace within chaos. In high school, I studied, won debate and speaking contests, wrote papers and spent hours at the library, often skipping class to do so. I became a Buddhist and meditated avidly. Trying to understand myself and meet my parents' expectations exasperated me. They wanted a social extrovert. I was a quiet introvert. They wanted me to be well-rounded, so they sent me to lessons: ballet, piano, swimming, ballroom dance. I failed them all. I was studious and creative.

I was given little opportunity to make my own decisions, handle money or discover the natural consequences of my actions. The family dynamic was Mother's illness/control, a workaholic Father, token communication and overbearing authoritarianism. This damaging combination ultimately led me to desperation. I left home the hard way.

After high school graduation, I disappeared in the night on a Vespa motor scooter with the buddy of a friend – a boy I didn't even know. I left my parents a note. I expressed my feelings about being taken for granted as the "built-in" babysitter, my desire for independence and a better opportunity for the education I craved. My mother took it as a personal affront (*How could I hurt her like that?*). My father worried it would wreck his business reputation.

1980s–1990s – California and Washington

I visit Mom.

Resolutely train yourself to attain peace. – Buddha

It was decades before I attempted to improve my relationship with my parents or cultivated the skills to do so. As time passed, my father became more neutral about me; he was busy expanding his business. My mother and I corresponded and visited occasionally. Later, after he passed, I made a point of visiting her to know her better and heal our misunderstandings. Our visits typically developed like this:

We sat at the table, cleared from dinner, dished stacked in the sink for later. I'd come to visit her again to try to heal our relationship. I longed to find something we had in common and to feel closer. We disagreed on almost everything. I tried to think of a friendly way to start our conversation.

"That was a great feast you made tonight with the fresh crab from Maureen's crab pots. Delicious! I love fresh seafood and living in the Central Valley doesn't give me the options you have here."

"Thank you. It was good, wasn't it? Almost gourmet. It was a treat for me too. It all depends on how the catch is and who has company that day. She's been very generous. We used to have crab pots when Dick had his little rowboat, but that was a while ago. What are you up to this evening?"

"I thought we could visit and catch up. That's what I came for."

"Well, that's a nice thought. I guess we could do that." She settled back in her chair, lit a cigarette, and sipped her leftover lukewarm coffee. Smoke curled upward toward the twenty-foot ceiling and drifted up the spiral stairs to the loft where I would sleep. I cringed. *Can't escape it I guess.*

"Why don't you tell me about your childhood?" I asked tentatively. "I'd love to hear your memories. You should write them down, you know."

She smiled. "I might do that for posterity. I'm not sure if you or your siblings would be interested. Perhaps your kids will be when they're old enough to think about such things. I guess I can remember . . ." She paused, staring into space, coffee cup in hand.

I mentally took note. Now I was worried. I shouldn't have started this. I thought it was an innocent question.

After a minute or two of silence, she continued. "Joyce [her sister] and I had a great childhood. We were absolutely inseparable. Life was so simple; you amused yourself. We played paper dolls for hours, using spice cans to make sofas and chairs. Some of the paper dolls were cutouts from magazines – in women's magazines there were pages of drawings of women wearing the fashions of the day. Later we made our own paper dolls.

"In the summer in Seattle, we used the piano as a home for these characters. We made up stories about them. We also loved to play with marbles – but not a real marble game. The pretty marbles were the girls and women, the ugly brown ones were the boys and men. We had a rug that had a pattern of many squares, and these squares were hotel rooms or houses for these marble people to live in.

"Our other favorite sport was roller-skating. We roller-skated almost seven days a week for nine months of the year. Mackie made clothes for Joyce and me during the summer, a lot of clothes. She made us "Sunday school dresses" which were white with a fine red check and with tiers of skirt – every summer she'd add another tier as we had grown in height."

I smiled. "That's cool. Thanks for sharing. You really should write this down. None of us know anything about your life."

"I'll think about that. It would take me a while – depending on how good my memory is that day." She paused, lifting her cup of now-cold coffee to her lips and sipping it. She put it down and continued.

"I just wish you had been more normal – more like me and Joyce. We had a lot of freedom as children. The world was different then. Mackie was much more of a mother to us. Mamma was always too busy with her students, practicing plays, and school activities. We did love the play rehearsals at the house but we didn't really have friends our age at home. We just amused ourselves and enjoyed the company – all the students and former students, and Mother's adult friends, like George and Gladys Savage, and Ben Weatherwax, who came to visit. It was always busy and social.

"You were an only child for a long time. You behaved strangely. Our neighbor, Mrs. Mitchell, declared you "old headed." She was right. I thought you'd be social, and play with other kids like we did. Instead you timidly refused to walk to the next block where there were lots of kids. I couldn't understand that. You didn't even play much with the kids next door – and there were five of them."

"Everybody is different."

"Yes, but not like you – you were so different – and difficult – as a child. Your dad and I had no idea what to do with you. We doted on you, though. Your grandparents [Dick's parents] did too. You were the first grandchild. Rusty [my paternal grandmother] and I made you all kinds of clothes; cute dresses, even coats. We took you everywhere we went in those days. You should have fond memories of that."

"Actually, I don't. I always felt left out. You visited your friends in the evening and played cards while I had to sleep on some stranger's bed, alone in a dark room. I felt abandoned. One day you forgot me at your friend's house after you finished playing badminton. You drove back later to get me. I stood in their driveway and cried. I was terrified. How could you do that?"

"Well, I don't know. It was a long time ago. I doubt we forgot you. You were a young child, you probably don't remember."

"I can't believe you'd say that. A lot of things scared me then. I was quiet and shy."

"Yes, you were. You hid under the table when it was time to open your birthday presents. You were scared of birthday candles and fireworks too. No normal child would act that way."

I crossed and uncrossed my legs. My left thigh felt stiff and my lower back ached. My stomach had squeezed itself into a hard rock. The crab felt like it was about to come up. My new, tight jeans pressed on my bloated stomach. I swallowed hard. My plan for us to talk and reach a peaceful understanding had failed again. I wanted to bolt for the door, and enjoy the quiet of the evening, the damp air of the beach. How many times had I visited her to heal old wounds, to really communicate? To become adult friends?

I forced myself to re-focus, take a deep breath, and start fresh.

"I was very shy until junior high school. There, I found great teachers who encouraged me to use my mind and self-discipline. I discovered I could excel in school and be recognized for my scholarship. I needed that encouragement to develop my abilities."

"You were so studious. Why? Couldn't you have been social, fun and friendly too? What's wrong with that? Do you remember the time you tried to play baseball while reading a book? You held the bat in one hand and the book in the other. What typical kid would have done that? I couldn't believe it. You were always different. We never understood you."

I took a few sips of water left from dinner and steeled myself. Resolutely, I continued. "Mom, I have a different type of personality, that's all. I'm studious. I love learning. I've studied many different disciplines – art, holistic healing, massage, philosophy, poetry – technical and practical disciplines, too. I love to read and experiment with what I learn. I have many stimulating friends and co-workers. I pursue my hobbies with passion. It's made me an interesting person. If you could be more open-minded, you'd understand that."

She sat up straight, put out her cigarette and crossed her arms defensively. "I love you, you're my daughter. And I've been a good mother to you. Gave you everything you needed."

"I didn't say you weren't. I'd just like us to listen and understand each other's point of view. We don't have to agree."

By now the air was filled with smoke. I was about to choke. The odor of the stale coffee nauseated me. My stomach gurgled loudly – a bad sign. I already felt sick, and our conversation wasn't going anywhere; at least not the way I'd hoped.

I stood up, pushed the chair in and pulled on my navy-blue sweatshirt. "Mom, I need to get some fresh air. I think I'll take a short walk on the beach and see you in the morning."

She turned to look at me, lifting her coffee cup again. "Well, have it your way. You always were stubborn just like you claim your father was. I'll be up for a while reading. See you in the morning."

10 ~ Personal Growth Ignites Change

Truth always repeats itself. You will hear the answers
from other sources until you can own it yourself.
–Tammy J. Holmes (Michael)

1950s–1980s – Washington and California

Growing up "Green" (a *Real Colors* personality type)

You are now aware that You decide who you are in every moment.
– Howard Falco, I AM

In junior high and high school, I was awkward, unattractive, and too smart for a girl. With no sense of how to be feminine or attractive, I wasn't a tomboy either. I didn't fit in. My mother provided little help. She probably didn't know what to do. She was undoubtedly worried that there was something "wrong" with me. In junior high school, when most girls were discovering boys, I barely knew they existed. I'd always felt it unfair that I wasn't a boy. I realized they had the advantage. They were my competitors.

She took the opportunity to talk to me on a Thursday evening in seventh grade while I was helping her prepare dinner. She turned to me as she arranged the thin-cut pork chops in the frying pan and said, "Are there any cute boys in your classes?"

I looked up at her blankly. "I don't know. I guess so." I continued to peel potatoes.

"Well," she resumed, "You're at the age now when you should be interested in boys."

I didn't know what to say, so I kept peeling.

"You know, God made two sexes for a reason."

I blushed, dropped the potato peeler on the counter and leaned toward the sink. I grabbed the faucet, turned the water on full and washed my hands. *What was coming next?* I didn't want to hear it.

She persisted. "I want to make sure you know that it's normal for girls your age to be attracted to boys."

I was dumbfounded. I had been selected the editor of the school newspaper. I had great teachers in English, art and history. They recognized my abilities and encouraged me to be the student I was capable of being. And she wanted me to be interested in *boys*? What was she thinking?

In high school I found a small clique of friends (the "Eggheads") who were intellectually curious, creative and unique souls. Finally, some people similar to me! I excelled in advanced classes and was on the debate team; we went to the state finals three years in a row. I won the student speaking contest for a local celebration. My parents were totally uninterested and uninvolved. I was never popular, rarely attended football games, never went to a prom. Like Minnie, I knew education was my ticket to freedom and independence.

I wanted to go away to college – to get as far away from my parents as possible, and pursue the education I craved. I thought I was scholarship material. There was no formal high school counseling for college planning. I knew I'd have to talk to Dad. Dinnertime was the best venue. The rain pounded, unrelenting, on the front window wall in the kitchen-dining area while the wind whipped through the tall Douglas fir trees surrounding the house. It was only 5:00 PM and already dark.

I helped Gail serve the baked ham with cinnamon raisin sauce, boiled potatoes, and green-bean casserole. The pungent smell of the ham complimented the sweet aroma of the raisin sauce, but together they couldn't overcome the overbaked, cheesy odor of the green beans. I turned my head as I set it on the table.

My siblings, five and seven years old, were already seated. They amused themselves by kicking each other under the table and giggling. "Stop it," Dick commanded sternly, as he sat down at the head of the table. "Settle down." His usual comment came after the first few bites. "What did you learn in school today?" He turned to me expectantly.

I put down my fork. "Dad, I got a 3.8 GPA again this semester. I think I could get a scholarship to a good school."

"Scholarship? What for? You don't need one to go to Western [Western Washington State College – now a university]. It's local, inexpensive and you could live at home. I'd be happy to pay for your tuition and books. If you didn't want to live here, you could work and support yourself."

I took a sip of milk while I pondered my answer. "I'd like to go away to college. There are many choices besides Western. I've started looking into some. The school counselor gave me the scholarship forms. If you'd fill them out, we'd know for sure if I could get one. It would be worth a try."

"Nonsense! My financial information is nobody's business. I don't share my finances with anyone besides your mother." He set his fork on his plate. He turned to look at Gail with a firm jaw and brash stare. She nodded silently in agreement, looked down at her plate and cut a bite of ham. He looked at me unsmiling. "I won't even consider it. It's Western or nothing."

There was no discussion allowed. My parents had no understanding of psychology or that young adults need to take part in decision-making to mature. Total lack of communication was one of the reasons I disappeared abruptly after graduation from high school; I was seventeen. Ultimately, my parents and Trudi, Mom's sister, agreed that I could stay at Trudi's home for the summer. This gave us an opportunity to work things out.

I spent the summer at "The Marble Factory," Trudi's home. She named it after the family myths about marbles. This included not only Mackie's winning T. J. as her husband in a bet with marbles, but Mackie and Minnie hiding marbles around Aberdeen and Hoquiam (and burying them in the freshly poured concrete sidewalks) "just for fun." Trudi always had a bowl of marbles on the narrow table by her kitchen window. She encouraged everyone to take one. If they visited again years later, marble in hand, she welcomed them back enthusiastically.

Trudi was a single parent, and her household was full of my cousins' friends as well as her own. Trudi was the mother I'd longed for – open-minded, fun, demonstrative and knowledgeable. She exhibited both Minnie's and Mackie's love of people and knack for socializing. Her home attracted educated, intellectual, artistic and musical friends. Many taught at the UW. I thrived during my short stay there.

By the end of summer, my family and I came to an agreement with our minister's expert guidance. In the fall, I went home and started art classes at Western. Within a year, I moved into an apartment with a girlfriend, supported myself, and explored my independence. My love of learning flourished under the direction of challenging, creative professors. I graduated with a B.A. in philosophy and a minor in art. I was the first woman to graduate in philosophy at Western.

Marriage, family and divorce

Change occurs because you want it to occur. – Neale Donald Walsch

David and I met in college. We married in 1966. I had already graduated; he was finishing his teaching degree. He was black; I was white. In Washington State, interracial marriage was legal. It was still illegal in seventeen states. The Supreme Court struck down anti-miscegenation laws the following year.

Marriage decreed my ultimate revolt. The more my parents discouraged it, the more determined I felt. I was pressured by both my husband-to-be and my parents. He wanted us to marry; they wanted no part of an interracial family. Torn between two extremes, I struggled with my decision. My future husband was similar to my parents: quick to anger, stubborn, and a rigid authoritarian. We'd both grown up in strict families and struggled with authority.

In retrospect, it was probably unlikely I'd pick anyone different from them. I'd been so protected, I hadn't experienced anything else. Since our new relationships mirror what we experience in childhood, and pose similar issues, I chose someone like them. They certainly didn't see it that way.

We were married in the Bellingham Unitarian Church. We wrote our own vows and planned our ceremony. My father disowned me. He and my brother didn't attend our wedding. Our marriage launched a complex dynamic of family issues that took over a decade to resolve – if they were ever resolved. My rebelliousness rose to new heights as we battled racial prejudice in our own unique ways. My paternal grandmother wrote me a letter lamenting my choices, expressing horror at the thought of our having children. She begged me not to perpetrate such a crime on a child. I never saw her again.

Both my husband and I struggled with multiple unresolved family issues from our childhoods. We also dealt with prejudice, social change and the chaos of the 1960s and '70s. Our marriage was tumultuous. We divorced after eleven years. I'd reached a point of being unable to handle so many issues any longer – at least those issues. I felt suffocated and didn't know how to cope. I had to generate a change – and hope it would be for the best.

We eventually came to peace over everything. It took a long time. Fortunately, we had three amazing children, two boys and a girl. In my typical individualistic way, and in keeping with our natural, holistic lifestyle, the first two were born at home using the Lamaze method of natural childbirth. I was attended by David and close friends. Veola, my second child and only daughter, was born on a sunny, warm February morning in Sacramento, California. She is the fifth generation that this book celebrates.

My parents had undoubtedly expected divorce. They were smart enough not to suggest it. A few years post-divorce, I took the children to my parents' home for Christmas where they met their paternal great-grandfather. He was charmed. Their paternal great-grandmother had passed as had both Minnie and Kling years earlier in my childhood.

My anxiety rose to new heights after my divorce. I felt overwhelmed by stress. I'd been a "homemaker" and out of the workforce for nine years. I had eighteen dollars in my checking account, a car with a dead battery and three hungry kids. The only food in the house was dried, preserved foods stored for emergencies. This wasn't the emergency I'd anticipated. I had to return to work; we couldn't live on the child support and alimony. A friend advised me to apply at Sacramento County. I landed a decent entry-level job right away. I also applied for and received daycare financial assistance. It was a new world for me and my family.

At my new county typist-clerk job, I sat at my desk in the back corner of a large office. I'd been on the job two weeks. I was nervous, adjusting to and learning my new routine. My supervisor, Susan, a long-time employee, walked toward my desk just before quitting time. "It's payday, Sheryl. Here's your first paycheck." She waved the blue envelope in the air. "I'm so glad you came to work with us at the County and I hope you'll have a long career here." She beamed as she handed it to me.

"Thank you. I hope so too." I smiled. I was happy with my job and thrilled to work in civil service. It had the benefits I needed as a single parent. I was eager for this paycheck and excited that I'd found a job so quickly. I felt confident now. I ripped open the envelope. When I saw the taxes, social security, health insurance and other deductions, my heart sank. I swallowed hard. My eyes filled with tears. *I can't believe it. My take-home pay isn't enough for us to live on.* I was shocked. Quickly I wiped my eyes, looked down and shuffled the paperwork on my desk, pretending to be busy. *What am I going to do now?*

11 ~ Embrace Your True Self

Be open-minded, but not so open-minded that your brains fall out.
– Bob Blees

1980s–1990s – California

My challenges as a re-entry woman

Imagine that your fear is coming from your inner child. Embrace it as a part of who you are.

In a few months, I was transferred to the downtown office as a clerk for the stationary (building) engineers. A great group of guys, they were thrilled to have my help with the start-up of the new county office building. I quickly realized they could support their families – and with their education, I could do their job. In a few months, I returned to school. Two years later, I graduated with an A.S. Degree in Mechanical-Electrical Technology and went to work in nuclear power electrical design as a technician. I became my family's breadwinner.

As a re-entry woman in the workforce, and having chosen a non-traditional job to earn the salary I needed, my anxiety accelerated with a whole new set of problems. Babysitters, time management, lingering poverty, a long commute with my carpool buddies, working overtime and dealing with sexism outside my immediate workgroup overwhelmed me. I still struggled with problems from my family of origin, too, as well as new issues of raising an interracial family alone in a predominantly white community. I knew I needed help.

Therapy – my quest for inner peace

Now I have my brush and colors. I just paint paradise and in I go.
– L. M., from our therapy group

One of my first therapy experiences was inner child work with our therapist Lisa, and a wonderful group of women. Together, we each explored our inner child in group therapy sessions. In *The Power of Your Other Hand*, Lucia Capacchione describes the inner child as "all our childlike feelings, instincts, intuitions, spontaneity and vitality. It is naturally open and trusting unless it learns to shut down for self-protection."[25] In our group, we shared feelings and experiences freely and honestly, helping each other heal our past.

John Bradshaw's popular books, workshops and PBS programs in the 1980s and '90s were the touchstone for my personal growth and healing. He explored issues including codependency, addiction, spirituality and emotional health. My big issue was shame. Bradshaw speaks of "toxic shame," a feeling of being a flawed or defective human being; a sense of worthlessness.[26] For me, shame developed out of the relationship with my mother. She was insecure and critical, and had unreasonably high standards. Possibly she wanted me to succeed where she couldn't, due to her anxiety and phobias. I was very similar to her. It was a recipe for failure.

In therapy, we learned to write with the non-dominant hand to access our inner child's feelings. By bringing them into adult consciousness, we released the emotions. Over time, they lost their charge. This also helped us overcome limiting beliefs. Lucia Capacchione wrote, "I have observed people using these techniques become more creative, expressive, and intuitive in their lives. . . . Many contact their spiritual source."[27]

In a journaling exercise, we wrote questions with the dominant hand (representing the adult; the conscious mind), and responded with the non-dominant hand (the inner child; the subconscious).

The questions and my inner child's answers were:

(Adult) What is your name and how old are you?
(Inner child) Sherry – twelve

(Adult) What does it feel like to be you?
(Inner child) Sad. Lonely. I wish I had a friend, a playmate. I'm so lonely. No one wants to play with me except sometimes grandpa.

(Adult) Tell me about yourself.
(Inner child) I'm holding the little stuffed dog that Hoppy's Aunt Betty brought back from Peru. [Betty Hopper was a student of Minnie's and family friend.] It's made with real llama hair and is so soft. I want to go there. I want to go away from here. I hate my family. They don't like me, they don't want me around. I am ugly, fat and awkward. The boys stare at me and I don't like it. I'm bigger than a lot of the other girls and boys. My parents tease me and embarrass me. No one likes me except my teachers. They say I'm smart.

(Adult) What happened to you?
(Inner Child) I don't know. I was born wrong. No one wanted me in the first place. They put me in the hospital and left me to die, but I didn't. I didn't do what they wanted from the beginning. I am wrong. Something – everything – is wrong with me but not with my sister. I made my parents sad by being me. I'm never okay. I'll never be okay to them. They tease me for being afraid.

(Adult) What would you like me to do for you?
(Inner child) Love me. Accept me. Let it be okay to be who I am with all my fears and insecurities. Tell me I'm beautiful. Play with me. I'm tired of playing alone.

The inner child's answers shocked me. I hadn't been aware of that part of myself for years. I now recognized how wounded I felt. It helped me understand my ongoing isolation. Those buried emotions took years to heal. I realized my fear came from my inner child. I learned to embrace it. From then on, any time I ignored my inner child, the feelings re-surfaced, reminding me to take better care of myself emotionally and spiritually. This healing experience taught me to parent myself with compassion and forgiveness; something we all need to do.

I'd used journaling for years to work through emotions, stress, fears and dreams. Non-dominant hand journaling provided a tool that ultimately led me to access my higher intuitive self. I found my own inner guidance through this method. I called it *SpiritWoman Speaks.*

Another therapy exercise helped us become aware of unwritten "family rules." This also came from Bradshaw's teaching. Every family has them. Typically they are an unconscious perpetration of our parents' patterns, learned in their families of origin, coupled with their own issues. We each develop our own interpretations of them. We accessed them using non-dominant hand writing.

For our family rules, I wrote:

Do not discuss religion.

Do not discuss sex.

Do not discuss money, especially not how much Dad made last year. "The Old Goat" [a business competitor of Dad's] might find out.

Do not discuss Mom's illness.

Do not discuss fears. They don't exist. Anything doesn't exist if we don't talk about it. Therefore nothing "bad" or hard to deal with exists. Problems do not exist.

It's OK to talk about having "fun," but don't do it. (I never could figure out what "go out and have fun" meant, which is what my mother still tells me to do. I still don't know how – I'm learning, though.)

You have to be home for dinner, sit at the table and sit in a certain way, with your legs next to each other, straight in front of you across the chair. Do not straddle it or stretch your legs out. Do not slouch. Do not speak unless spoken to.

Eat all the food on your plate. People are starving in India.

Do not discuss anything unless it is in an intellectual manner.

Do not express feelings – remember they don't exist if you don't express them (only good things exist).

Do not ask questions – at least not too many.

Dad has the final say and he is always right, ultimately. After all, he works hard and brings home the paycheck.

Don't "run around naked." [wear less clothing than appropriate]

Never go out of the house in curlers.

Don't wear slippers around the house.

These crazy-making, dysfunctional family rules foster fear and undermine independence, feeling, thinking and freedom. They create codependency, insecurity, shame. Codependency is the loss of selfhood. Holding on to the emotions that develop around this way of living and feeling creates fatigue, stress, and ill health. It requires effort on many levels to overcome.

Since my father was an only child from an abusive family, and my mother's parents divorced when she was in junior high, neither had a model for nourishing parenting or normal family life. They both had many unresolved personal issues. They couldn't be better parents. I totally understand and accept this now. I worked through my feelings of abandonment, anger and disappointment through therapy and the holistic healing modalities I embraced. I let the past go and became who I truly was.

Visualization – a new tool in my toolbox

The fundamental process of creative visualization is simply this – to imagine as clearly and realistically as possible what you want to happen. – Shakti Gawain

After divorce, additional schooling and a job in a nontraditional field, I'd come a long way. However, I still struggled with anxiety.

My major panic attacks centered on my children's safety, anxiety produced by my job, and finances. I'd read about positive imagery and visualization and their use in sports performance and healing. Could it work for me? I was determined to find out. I refined the process to fit my needs.

I sat silently in the evenings when the house was quiet and visualized situations that made me anxious. I imagined myself at work, and instead of feeling anxious, I felt confident and solved problems easily. I imagined my children safe at the babysitter's house, going on outings or playdates and returning home safely. I visualized excess money in my checking account and paying bills easily. I mentally added a few zeros to my checkbook balance to create a sense of abundance. I repeated these thoughts and visions many times until the emotional charge disappeared. I prayed that I would overcome my fears.

Self-help was my key. I realized I could fit what I learned to my situation and get results. I cured my anxiety. When I drove to and from work alone, I spoke my mantra aloud: "You can do this, Sheryl." I still use it today.

A minister once told me that any positive mantra will work if it's simple, easy to remember and you repeat it with emotion. In order for visualization or affirmations to be effective, we must access the subconscious mind and plant the suggestion with feeling. This works best in a relaxed, alpha state. In *The Power of Your Subconscious Mind*, Joseph Murphy says that the conscious mind is submerged when in a drowsy state, so ideas are more readily accepted.[28]

Voice dialogue – psychology of the selves

I remodeled my inner parent to become the compassionate parent I needed.

In later therapy, I learned about the concept of different selves within the psyche. This idea is rooted in Transactional Analysis, Jungian concepts, Gestalt Therapy and Psychodrama. These inner selves can be the Inner Parent, the Vulnerable Child, the Controller/Protector and many others. Psychologists Hal and Sidra Stone developed Voice Dialogue, a therapy method in which inner drama is worked out by accessing and playing out the roles of different inner selves, each of which has its own voice inflection, gestures and emotions. This helped me understand and embrace the non-acceptable parts of myself and integrate them. It was an additional tool in my self-help toolbox.

Scenario Role Playing shatters emotional barriers.

Any questions, comments, gripes, complaints, criticisms, testimonials, confessionals, unresolved emotions, bad dreams, or unpaid invoices? – Bob Blees's litany prior to every session

I was tense when I attended my first role-playing workshop. Lisa, my therapist, had strongly recommended it. I knew it would challenge, change, and scare me. It did. But I felt committed and attended with some of the women in my therapy group. It was "safety in numbers" for us.

The workshop was held over a three day weekend. While the group was gathering, chatting and enjoying snacks, I noticed Bob Blees, our therapist and facilitator, perusing the room with his penetrating, insightful gaze. Finally, he scrutinized me. I squirmed and looked away. My palms immediately became sweaty. I felt the knot growing in my stomach. As he called the group together, he singled me out. "What would you say if I told you that you didn't belong here today, you were wasting your time trying to change and develop new reactions to emotionally-charged situations?"

Apparently he already knew how to push my buttons. I sat up straighter, looked him boldly, and defensively blurted out, "I'd say, 'Fuck you!' " Everyone burst into laughter. The tension that had hung over the room released instantly. I found I did belong there. I learned new techniques for relating to people and diffusing stressful situations while being true to myself and respectful of others. This was huge for me.

Bob developed his unique method by constructing roles from his clients' life experiences. Each role was a simulated life conflict that mimicked confrontations typical of family life, work environments and personal relationships. We were given background information about our parts, our perspective on the situation to be enacted, and information on the other roles. The goal was to take care of ourselves emotionally while resolving the conflict. This provided an opportunity to "try out" different responses to emotionally-charged situations. It allowed us to practice thinking, feeling and acting in more constructive ways; the best way to learn new behaviors.

The scenarios were played by members of the group in two sets (groups A and B) who had no knowledge of the other group's resolutions. Each role-playing group was composed of around a half dozen people who performed the role in front of the remainder of the group (except for those in the second or "B" role, who were sequestered in another room). The results were amazing.

Bob (who was a minister) always jokingly said that the three-day workshop started with the crucifixion on Friday and worked up to the resurrection by Sunday. He was right. Easier roles were played first and progressed in difficulty throughout the workshop. We noticeably developed more kindness, self-understanding and ability to manage our emotions as the weekend progressed. I still vividly remember many of the roles I played, what I felt and how I responded. It astounded me that one of the roles I played "came to life" in my personal experience later. The roles I enacted are as real to me today as experiences in all other areas of my life. Role playing significantly changed my life for the better.

1990s–2010s – Arizona and California

Individuals who identify themselves as a green personality style actually do their best work alone. – Real Colors

Do you know your "Real Colors?"

The Real Colors personality-type evaluation is a popular team-building tool often used by corporations. It's touted as the "modern" Myers-Briggs personality assessment. It divides the population (generally equally between men and women) into four personality types or temperaments: gold, orange, blue and green.

The golds are the super achievers; dependable, organized, well-prepared and good at implementing plans. They get things done. The oranges are adventurers who need to be free and spontaneous. They are enthusiastic, love to try new things, take risks and achieve visible results. The blues feel concern for others and value authenticity. They are good listeners, peacemakers, and accept others. They often find their calling in helping professions. Greens are logical, objective thinkers. They are inquisitive and prefer to work independently. They value competency. Everyone has all the colors represented in their temperament spectrum. Most people have one or two colors or sets of traits that are predominant.[29]

I'm a mental and emotional adventurer, but sometimes I prefer to be well-prepared. I looked up the assessment tool on-line and took the test before the workshop at my job. The results confirmed what I intuitively knew. I was a green. The workshop assessment was an expanded version of what I'd found on-line.

When we received our results, we were divided into our color groups. I was shocked. The other greens in my very small group were people I'd worked with for quite a while but found difficult to know, understand and relate to. They weren't "touchy-feely." *Oh my God, I must appear this way to others too.*

In the next exercise, each group completed a poster-board sheet to share with the others. We were to elaborate on four significant areas: values, needs, joys and strengths. This provided our teambuilding tools. I selected a green marker, and we met in the foyer of the workshop room.

"Well, let's see. This is easy for us." Sal took the marker and wrote the heading, "Green" and the four qualities we were to describe. We completed our task in less than ten minutes.

We wrote:

> Values: Independence
> Needs: Being challenged
> Joys: Learning (education)
> Strengths: Ingenious

Greens cut to the chase. The other groups filled their sheets with lists, symbols, pictures. Each color group had a telling style typical of their thinking. Golds wrote theirs in an elaborate prioritized list. Blues had no title, and their words, symbols and pictures were drawn in many colors all over the sheet, including their typical heart symbol. There were no oranges in our workgroup, but one of the facilitators was an orange. Her sparse chart depicted some stick figures and a few symbols.

I quickly embraced my green coworkers. Their challenges were *my* challenges. I finally understood why my blue co-workers acted hurt when I spoke brusquely, factually and unemotionally. I learned how to get along with different temperaments. It was life-changing. And after all that therapy, too!

Statistics of the US population show that golds are the majority (40-45%), split equally between male and female (M/F), oranges are next with 30-35%, also split also split equally between M/F; blues come in third with 15-20%, split M/F 40/60; and greens come in last at 5-10%, split M/F at 60/40.[30]

My father was a green. He was an architect, had his own business, designed and built much of his own home, loved to work and solve challenging problems. Our birthdays are one day apart. We both always wondered why we weren't closer. A lot of it was our personalities. Greens are not emotional or overly affectionate. They are matter-of-fact and prefer emotionally simple relationships.

My mother was a combination of blue and orange. She was hypersensitive, emotional and insecure. She experimented with many ideas and hobbies, from playing guitar to Tarot reading. She always doubted her competency. She was a mental adventurer. She did write to-do lists (we all did) but stuck with something only as long it stimulated her intellectually. I am similar in that way.

Can we really make positive, lasting changes in our personalities? I know we can. My experience with therapy, prayer, breathwork, meditation and other holistic techniques testifies to that. To make positive changes permanent, I found it's helpful to know ourselves and what works best for us, as well as understanding the science behind the method. Realistically, though, we often need to experiment and have faith in God or a Higher Power that we'll be led to our bliss. Faith, patience and practice are crucial to positive change.

Veola Vazquez, my daughter, is a child psychologist, professor, author, wife and mother. She enjoys writing middle-grade novels, women's fiction, devotionals, and blogs. She is a sought-after inspirational speaker at Christian women's retreats and other events.

She invokes the power of Jesus Christ and Christ-consciousness in passages from her devotional below.

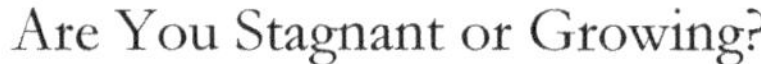

Are You Stagnant or Growing?

2 Corinthians 5:17 – "Therefore, if anyone is in Christ, the new creation has come: The old has gone, the new is here!"

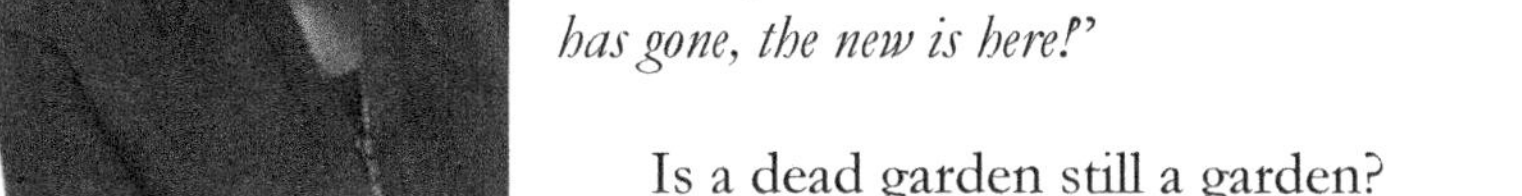

Is a dead garden still a garden?

Veola Vazquez, Ph.D.

I asked myself that question after I planted my own personal nursery a short time ago. Imagine this: three-foot high planters filled with the best soil. Seedlings gently placed in straight rows. Water and sunshine. The perfect ingredients for blossoms, the smell of herbs and fresh fruit and veggies. Spring was coming!

But nothing grew. They weren't dead, but something was missing. They were firmly planted but had not matured.

Doesn't that sound like the Christian walk at times? We can be firmly planted in our faith but fail to grow, fail to become more like Christ. We become stagnant despite being told to never stop growing and to bear fruit.

Being stagnant is never a good thing. If you think about things that are stagnant – where change and growth do not occur – it's usually negative. . . . Becoming "stagnant" is an insidious process. It doesn't happen overnight. The day-to-day busyness, stress, conflict, or difficulties of our lives often crowd out our relationship with Christ. It is easy to place God last on our "to-do" list. When we do, we stop moving in the direction of growth. And we may not even notice it happening.

If you find yourself stagnant, is there something you can do to change it? "Can people really change?" I believe they can. Second Corinthians 5:17 tells us we can. But new hearts and new lives mean new behaviors. Sometimes that's easier said than done.

Nothing good comes without time and hard work. Bearing fruit involves being pruned and weathering the elements of our lives in a Christ-like fashion. What kind of fruit are we to bear as believers? Galatians 5:22-23 tells us: *the fruit of the Spirit is love, joy, peace, longsuffering, kindness, goodness, faithfulness, gentleness, self-control.* Unlike raising tomatoes and eggplant, cultivating this kind of fruit can be a challenge. It takes a choice. It means using loving words with a spouse who may not do the same in return. It means caring for that irritating co-worker. Above all, it means clinging to Christ's promise to give you a new life.[31]

1970s–1990s – California and Washington

I have lived with several Zen masters – all of them cats. –Eckhart Tolle, The Power of Now

Not wanting to stagnate, I continued to embrace new challenges. While I raised my family and learned about myself, my family of origin moved on. I had little to do with them for decades. We lived three states apart; not far in distance but worlds away in understanding. First as a wife and mother, and ultimately as a single parent, I was unstoppably busy.

My brother and sister grew up in the 1970s. Geoff was in a band, *West Coast Brass*, with his neighbor, Rick, and some other friends. They often practiced in the large basement of the family home. Starr was doing multi-media light shows with her boyfriend, Jim, around the Pacific Northwest and at Western for Professor Bishop.

The family home, 205 Middlefield Road, Bellingham, WA, 1970s

Gail became a Master Gardener in the first official class. She developed her skills in writing, crafts, music and gardening. Determined to get published, she stayed up late at night, writing. She still excelled at humor, as she had in her prize-winning high school essay. She continued to submit her short stories to popular magazines. She quipped, "I'm collecting rejection slips." An inveterate cat lover, she always had a couple around to keep her company as she sat up alone at night to write. The black ones were her favorites. She describes them in this story from the early 1970s.

How to Distinguish Between Two Black Cats

People always say, "Oh – you have *two* black cats. They look just alike – how do you tell them apart?" To a cat lover, this is about as reasonable as asking how to tell your children apart. Actually, it's a matter of looking but not seeing.

Gooey has fifteen left whiskers and seventeen right whiskers, spaced close together, very fine and hard to count even against a background of newspaper while she's napping on it. Her left eyebrow has four long hairs, and there are seven in the right. Inside each ear is a tuft of stiff, thick, white hairs, thirteen left and eleven right, very short and not noticeable unless you are checking black cats for white-haired ears. They look like skin at a distance. Baby Cat's ears are hairless. His eyebrows are short, five left hairs, three right. His whiskers are thick, crisp and widely-spaced, fourteen left and twelve right, counted against a dark bedspread.

Since the living-dining-kitchen areas are all one space, if you're a guest you'll notice (particularly if we're cooking) that one cat is sitting on the dining table and one on the counter. Instead of uttering disgusting cries of alarm (as squeamish people do), you might just take note: Baby Cat rests on the table; Gooey perches on the counter. If Gooey is staring into the sink, she's thirsty. She is finicky about not drinking stagnant waters – she has to see it poured. Outside, this bias disappears; any murky puddle will do. Baby Cat prefers to drink from running faucets or hoses, but will actually settle for anything including coffee dregs or martini remainders.

There are other important differences too. Baby Cat's tail is stiff and easily measured; it's an even twelve inches. Gooey's tail – soft, fluid and expressive – is harder to measure. When you think you have it captured, it has slithered away. It's about eleven or twelve inches. Just remember – stiff one on Baby, wavy one on Gooey.

Girth, equidistant from front and rear legs, is easy. Gooey is fourteen inches and Baby seventeen and one half. Gooey's skin is not full – it is quite loose; Baby Cat's skin is a good fit.

Weight is significant if you enjoy picking up strange cats. Getting a cat to step on a scale is hardly worth the effort unless you're spending idle time when snowed in. I simply get on the scale with and without the cat and subtract the difference. With Gooey, I weigh six pounds more and with Baby, eleven. When you pick up Baby Cat, you dig in your heels.

When you pick up Gooey, she flops and sags and both ends, like the partially de-feathered pillows we used as children at grandmother Mackie's house; the feathers immediately seem to fly as she makes her escape. Baby Cat is a very satisfactory object to pick up – a living beanbag. He can be draped over your shoulder, wrapped around your neck (if you tolerate eleven-pound neck scarves), turned upside down or squeezed playfully. He relishes having his paws crossed or his nose tickled with his tail. If you turn him on his back and rock him, he will close his eyes, smile and purr.

If you lie on the sofa, Baby Cat will be waiting; a cozy, firm and willing pillow. And if you haven't tried a vibrating pillow, it is worth the experiment. Gooey prefers you to be the pillow. But don't pet her – she has a strong tendency to drool when happy. Yes, she's gooey.

If you are here to jam with the band (which lots of our visitors are) or just happen to show up when the band is in the basement, you'll know who's who. Gooey can sleep through the whole practice, but prefers that an LPB-1 power booster not be used. Wah-wah pedals make her ears twitch. Baby gets out fast. He even dislikes our favorite FM station, but will tolerate Nilsson and Chet Atkins records, or live piano playing.

Gooey plays piano at night. It's usually about midnight, just before she retires. She's patiently waited at the sink for her bedtime water. Then she prances across the counter divider to the living room side, and steps down onto the piano bench. She strolls back and forth leisurely on the piano keys. At the risk of being thought crazy, I'd swear she knows what she's doing.

She is a day cat. If you happen to relish stirring up your blood with morning dancing to Tom Rush records (doesn't everybody?), she's prepared. She races through the house and jumps at you in passing, or hides behind chairs waiting to pounce. Baby's on the other schedule – he rests by daylight because he's busy rolling golf balls or playing with anything he can find at night, creating as much racket as possible.

Are you still in doubt about which cat is which? Gooey has white patches under her chin and on her stomach. Oddly enough, no one seems to notice.

12 ~ Thoughts Create Your Reality

Personal power is the ability to live authentically in each moment.
– Synthia Andrews, *The Path of Energy*

1960s–1970s – Boston, Massachusetts and California

Macro-what?

Not-knowing is true knowledge.
Presuming to know is a disease.
First you realize that you are sick;
then you can move toward health.
– *Tao te Ching*

Holistic health practices were not mainstream when I embraced them in the 1960s. I was ahead of my time. I learned early in life that health was everything. I'd always been a spiritual seeker; it came naturally to me. I embraced new disciplines, both spiritual and physical, to boost my health and happiness.

Billed by a women's magazine in the 1960s as *The Diet That's Killing Our Kids*, the macrobiotic ("great life") diet was a revelation to me. I thrived on it. Macrobiotic concepts were introduced to the West by George Ohsawa (1893–1966). He studied ancient Asian medicine based on the concept of Yin and Yang (opposing yet complementary energetic forces) related to the traditional Japanese diet. His goal? Develop a diet that produced optimum health and longevity.

Early in our marriage, my husband and I sought greater health and extended life. Strange for a couple in their twenties? Perhaps it was one of the energetic forces that brought us together. We studied macrobiotics with Michio and Aveline Kushi in Boston, and with Herman and Cornelia Aihara in Sacramento. We learned and later taught the principles and practice of macrobiotics: food selection and cooking, massage, and the ancient philosophy of Yin/Yang energy interaction. Macrobiotic practice at the time was primarily a strict brown rice and vegetarian diet, often considered a dangerous cult. Macrobiotic principles remain the same but the practice has become more holistic over time.

We visited my mother after our major diet change. Due to our interracial marriage and incompatible lifestyles, we'd seen very little of my parents. We parked in the driveway and entered through the modern carport of Dad's Frank Lloyd Wright-inspired home. We walked across the well-crafted wooden deck lined with pots of red geraniums. I knocked on the sliding glass door. Mother opened the door, standing stiffly in her gray slacks and a striking red-and-black shirt.

She greeted us cautiously. "Hello. Come in and sit down. I'm glad you stopped by."

We walked in. David shook her hand firmly and greeted her with a smile. "It's nice to see you again."

"Let me get you some coffee." She motioned for us to sit down.

She opened the cupboard and took out coffee cups and saucers. The powerful smell of freshly brewed coffee wafted into our nostrils as we perched on their modern, uncomfortable chairs.

I responded, "No thanks. We don't drink coffee anymore."

She walked around the divider between the kitchen and living area. She crossed her arms and looked at me suspiciously.

"You don't drink coffee? What normal person doesn't drink coffee?" She turned back to the coffee and poured a cup.

I persisted. "It's not good for us, Mom. We're on a healthy diet now. I feel a lot better. My intestinal problems are gone."

She stepped out from behind the divider again. "I can't believe you don't drink coffee. Everyone drinks coffee. You used to drink it with cream and sugar."

"We follow a traditional Asian diet now. It's much healthier. Coffee isn't good for us. White sugar is a killer. Dairy products aren't healthy either. Around seventy-five percent of the world's population is lactose intolerant. Cow's milk is for calves."

She walked toward me, glowering. Her green glasses slid down on her nose. She looked over them and held up her coffee cup menacingly.

"I don't understand. I offer you coffee and you refuse. I'm trying to be polite. No daughter of mine ever refused coffee."

She stepped back into the kitchen, put down the cup, shoved the remaining coffee cups into the cupboard and yanked the cabinet's accordion-fold door shut. We rose hastily and walked to the door. I thanked her quietly and pulled the slider shut behind us as we left.

est (Erhard Seminars Training) – "Did you get it?"

I find myself and my own reality.

My earliest exploration into my personal unknown was with *est* (Erhard Seminars Training) in San Francisco, in the early 1970s. In two experiential weekends of sensory deprivation, and being shouted at by the trainer ("Get off it! You're all assholes!"), I was forced to face parts of myself I didn't know existed. Confronting fear was my nemesis.

We couldn't wear watches, were locked in an ice-cold room with 200 other people (it was "our choice"), couldn't sit by anyone we knew, speak unless called upon, or take notes. We weren't allowed to go to the bathroom or eat except on formal, infrequent breaks (participants with medical conditions were exempt and sat in the back row). We went through "Processes" designed to force us out of our safe, controlled egos, roles, paradigms, acts and habits. The intention was to free ourselves of past, recurring, non-working patterns. Through these experiential processes, we confronted our lack of aliveness. *Est* widely introduced the concepts of personal transformation and taking responsibility for your life.

The training's purpose was to enable us to transform our experience so situations that we'd tried to change or continued to tolerate would clear up automatically in the process of living. We were told we were perfect as we were, and asked if we "got it?" "It" was the result of the training; our ability to experience the present moment fully ("be here now"), and accept who we were ("love what is") without clinging to the past, being stuck in a point of view, or reacting like a robot due to childhood programming. It was an attempt to replicate enlightenment.

All the processes were challenging, but the Fear Process shook me to the core. We were herded into an open area in the ballroom and given barf bags in case we threw up during the process. The trainers walked around yelling instructions.

"Everyone lie down on the floor and close your eyes. Imagine you are an actor or actress. Imagine you are afraid of the person next to you. You have every reason to be afraid. Feel it, believe it. Everyone around you makes you more fearful. The person next to you is afraid too. You are more afraid than you were a minute ago. Now you, yourself are the most frightening person in the room. Everyone is afraid of *you.* You frighten everyone around you. Everyone here is terrified."

I lay uncomfortably on the cold floor. Within minutes, my whole body was freezing and rigid. My breath caught in my throat. *Oh my God, I'm going to stop breathing.* I panicked. My heart raced. I couldn't move. I heard someone next to me throwing up. Instinctively, I clutched my stomach. I felt nauseated and heaved into the bag. Nothing came up. People were sobbing uncontrollably. My nerves and skin felt raw. My legs jerked and I trembled violently. *I'm going to die.* I pulled myself into the fetal position, arms covering my head. The noise of everyone screaming and sobbing petrified me, sending me further into pure terror. *I can't escape.* My panic attack lasted the entire session.

By the time we got out around 1:00 AM, I could barely function. I stared blankly into space as I followed David to the car. I felt numb all over. I couldn't think. I was in a daze for weeks.

As a result of the training, I realized I needed to overcome fear, understand myself better, and make peace with my parents. I had no idea how. This was the first time I'd confronted myself, my fears, and the result of our family dysfunction.

The Silva Method astonishes me.

A trained mind is more powerful.

The Silva Method was the next stop on my journey. It facilitated development of my intuitive and psychic abilities, training me to strengthen and focus both my intuition and rationality. In my opinion, the Silva method is a form of hypnosis (Jose Silva, the founder, studied it). The word was never used. When I took the class in the '70s, it taught guided imagery techniques, meditation, habit control, and mental programming for enhanced health. It facilitated self-healing and remote viewing using positive suggestions and focused visualization while in alpha and theta brain-wave states. I'm not familiar with their current processes; they may have been updated since I took the training.

Their website today advertises that over six million people in 110 countries have been trained since 1966 (the year Silva went public with the training). Their curriculum uses a combination of alpha and theta level mind exercises, habit control, visualization and positive programming. They report that people using their method are often able to manifest greater habit control and command over emotions and life situations. Their work has been verified by a number of research instututions.[32] However, controversy has ensued over whether their methods are scientifically-based. It will be interesting to see how this plays out as brain science develops.

I can still hear our trainer, Evan, leading us in exercises. His mellifluous voice helped me relax me as he counted down slowly from ten to one, a typical hypnotic induction technique. He continued, "You are now at a deeper, healthier level of mind." I felt peaceful and relaxed. He instructed us, "Keep your right hand in your lap and drop your left hand down by your side. Imagine your hand is immersed in a bucket of ice water.

"Feel your hand and arm getting cold now. Feel the ice cubes with your fingers, sense how slick and cold they are. Feel the cold water touching your hand and wrist. Imagine the water just got colder. The bucket is filled with ice. Your hand is getting colder now, your wrist is cold. You shiver. Sense the coldness in your fingertips; your skin absorbs the chill. It's so cold you are losing sensation in your hand. Feel it. Experience it now."

I sat silently on the hard folding chair in a class of twenty-five in the dimly lit meeting room. My hand became colder, immersed in the imaginary bucket of ice water. This went on for an indeterminate length of time. At that level of mind there is no time consciousness. Evan continued, "I will now count from one to five. On the count of one, you will bring your hand out of the bucket and place it on your lap. "One, two . . . five. Eyes open now, wide awake. Your left hand is numb and icy with no sensation in your fingertips. Your right hand is warm, and feels normal."

I felt my hands. He was right. My left hand was ice cold. My fingers were stiff. My entire left arm and shoulder felt chilled as if I'd just emerged from an ice cave. My right hand and arm felt warm and normal.

I was stunned. If my own mind could do that, what else could it do?

1980 – Bordeaux, France and Washington State

Dick experiences a health crisis.

The only thing that ever prevents your receiving something that you desire is that your habit of thought is different from your desire.
– Esther and Jerry Hicks (Abraham)

While I raised my family and learned about myself, major changes occurred for my aging parents. In the summer of 1980, my uncle, Jud, (Gail's brother) gave his second French cooking-school course in Bordeaux, France. The school was taught in English and the audience American. An attorney professionally, he was also a gourmet cook. He taught cooking classes in his home, and wrote articles on cooking and wine for the local Longview newspaper as well as national newspapers and magazines.

My brother lived in Munich at the time, so he picked up our parents and they attended the last week of the school together. My dad, Dick, had a cold or sinus infection that week. After they flew home, he became ill and was diagnosed with cerebral meningitis (inflammation of the membrane covering the brain).

He was hospitalized for a short time, treated with antibiotics and sent home. Within a couple of days he became very ill and returned to the hospital. He had a cerebral hemorrhage. He was in a coma for thirty-five days in the ICU, and in the hospital for six weeks. He never fully recovered from the resulting memory loss.

Gail cared for him for ten years. He was able to function and perform basic care needs, walk the dog, read, watch TV. His memory for more complex activities was severely diminished. His social skills were also limited. He experienced severe bouts of anger and frustration regarding his situation.

During this ordeal, Gail struggled with her grief and loss. Her Christian Science background had taught her that he could get well. He responded with anger and resistance. The doctors confirmed that this was to be expected due to the type and location of his brain injury. As a man who'd been competent in many areas, and who now couldn't recall how to play a cassette tape, he had every reason to be angry.

c. 1985 – Sandy Point, Ferndale, Washington

Gail struggles with her beliefs.

A word is a treatment. – Emma Curtis Hopkins

Gail's new lifestyle as Dick's caregiver challenged her. Her daily routine started with convincing him to take his medications.

"Okay, papa, it's 8:00 AM and time for your medicines. I have them all here for you – the blood thinner, and all the rest – you have so many now I don't even remember what they're all for."

"Huh? Just give me my orange juice. That's all I want right now."

"No. You have to take these pills too. Here, I'll help you. Here's the Coumadin." She handed it to him.

He took the pill and looked at it blankly. "What's this for? I don't need it."

"Yes you do, it's your blood thinner. Just take it now." She handed him his juice.

"Hmmm . . . okay, I guess." He gulped it down with half the juice. "I think I'll take a walk." He pushed his chair back from the table.

"Wait, you have three more to take. Here." She handed him the pills.

"Oh, all right. Get off my back, will you?" He swallowed the pills with the remaining juice, got up and walked to the door.

"You need your jacket."

"Oh, I forgot." He headed back through the living room to the closet, but opened the laundry room door instead. "I don't see a jacket in here. Where's the closet?" He turned, confused.

"Right behind you."

He grumbled, "God damn it," turned, yanked open the door and took out his dark-gray windbreaker.

"You know if you'd just think *closet across from the laundry room* you'd probably remember where it was."

"I don't need your help. Leave me alone." He slammed the closet door and put on his windbreaker.

She walked toward him. "You could be more positive. Just say, 'Thank you. I'll remember it next time.' Thoughts are things. Your thoughts create your own reality, you know."

He glared down at her. "I don't care. I don't want to hear it. I'm going outside now." He pulled his fuzzy, gray stocking cap from the pocket and put it on. He zipped up his jacket, turned abruptly, walked past her to the slider, pulled it open and stepped out into the brisk wind. He breathed in the salt air gratefully and let out a long sigh. *Just what I need.* He walked across the deck to the beach, watching the reflected light dance on the waves as they splashed on the damp sand.

Gail coped with her own anxiety, physical ailments and frustration, as well as his. She asked me and my siblings to use our own versions of prayer, positive thought and energy healing to help him. We did; he improved. Unfortunately, it wasn't significant enough for him to become who he'd been before the brain injury.

His illness tested Gail's convictions. She returned to her Christian Science roots. It wasn't the Christian Science that Mary Baker Eddy preached or that Mackie taught by example. It was the basic philosophic principles. Gail was not religious. She believed in God or a Higher Power and questioned everything else.

She shared her beliefs with my cousin in a letter:

> *I am answering hastily the same day I got your letter because otherwise it will be lost forever. When I have the time, I will get you the book that has become my philosophy. It is called The Power of Your Subconscious Mind and I have a funny feeling I told you about it last time I wrote. Or did I? I don't know what the Hell I've done. Yes, I believe that you have to be absolutely positive – this book will explain all the ways.*
>
> *When you read this book you just remove the word "God" which always gives me the creepy-crawlies and substitute something else – "universal mind" or just "subconscious," or a lot of other things. I think what you think is what you get, so you have to have faith and keep repeating to yourself morning and night and during the day all the good things you expect.*
>
> *This book really got me through those six hospital weeks. Every time a doctor would tell me some dire thing that might happen I would point at him and say firmly, "NO!" There was only one that took offense at my attitude; all the others understood. In fact, one said, "You must have read the book, How to be a Bigger Man." I said, "No, it was The Power of Your Subconscious Mind." We both laughed.*

In *The Power of Your Subconscious Mind*, author Joseph Murphy shared "six practical techniques in mental healings." All are effective and use different approaches. His "Affirmative method" is similar to Christian Science although not based on the Bible in the same way. He stated: "The effectiveness of an affirmation is determined largely by your understanding of the truth and meaning that underlie the words, *in praying use not vain repetition*. The power of your affirmation lies in the intelligent application of definite and specific positives. . . . To affirm is to state that it is so."[33]

Mother knew in her heart that the power of thought could heal her husband. She tried everything to convince him. In her frustration, she badgered him to change. He was unable to. Over time, he improved some. He still had a sense of humor, could carry on a conversation, and be his former delightful self. However, a part of his brain had been gravely injured, resulting in limited memory and functionality. He sometimes declared angrily that he'd already read the paper when he first picked it up off the porch, or had seen a TV program before it aired. Perhaps he was investigating the next world even then.

13 ~ Your Truth is Valid

If you are depressed you are living in the past.
If you are anxious you are living in the future.
If you are at peace you are living in the present.
– Lao Tzu

1990s–2000s – California

Gail copes with grief; I deal with our relationship.

There is nothing to heal – only an idea to change.
– Science of Mind Asilomar Retreat 2007

On a typical workday morning at the Rancho Seco Nuclear Generating Station, I sat at my desk in the corner of a large area that had once been the instrument shop. I sipped hot peppermint tea while I planned my day. The commitment database needed updating. I had a meeting at 1:00 PM to report on our progress in meeting local and federal decommissioning requirements. The phone rang with two short rings; an outside call. I picked up the receiver. "Good morning, this is Sheryl."

I heard a cough and muffled sneeze. "Your father died in his sleep last night." My mother's voice was flat. "It was totally unexpected. Your sister is coming from Seattle and she'll handle the arrangements. I'll call your brother next."

I sat numb, stunned. There'd been no change in his condition for months. I stammered, "I . . . I'm sorry, Mom. What happened? How can I help?"

After a long silence she spoke slowly. "I don't know right now. Your sister will call you. I can't talk. I can't even think. I went into his bedroom this morning because he hadn't gotten up. He was dead. Cold. I panicked and called 911. They came, told me he'd passed in the night. He had a normal evening, reading in his chair. He felt fine when he went to bed. Please call me tonight. You can talk to your sister then, too."

"I will. I'm so sorry. You're sure there isn't anything I can do?"

"No, I don't think so."

"Okay, I'll call you tonight. Love you."

I hung up the phone. Dazed, I slumped forward and stared at the computer screen. Everything seemed to slow down. I tried to think or feel anything. I only felt lost. I blinked several times, trying to focus. I pictured Dad as he'd been when he was young and in vibrant health, laughing, talking, joking, interested in everything, picking up rocks on the beach and explaining how they'd been formed. He'd been an amateur geologist.

Suddenly I sensed something. A subtle energy enveloped me. I held very still, sensing it surround me. I felt as if he were there, reassuring me somehow. That it was all right, it was best, he'd moved on. A feeling of stillness and calm flowed through my heart. Then I cried. As I wiped my tears, a sense of relief passed through me. I realized he was at peace now. I hoped that Mom could find peace, too.

Dick died in October 1991. He was seventy-three. Gail sold their Sandy Beach home around a year after he died. She moved into an apartment on Bellingham's south side where the family home had been. It was much later that she shared her feelings about grief in a letter. When she wrote, she usually had a "signature of the day" which mimicked her mood. It was often "Nervous Nellie;" today it was just "Nellie."

First Thursday in March '93

Hi –

I'm afraid my communication skills are failing these days. I was surprised to discover that you thought I was suffering and miserable. Since you are a contemplative and introspective person, I just thought you might find it interesting to hear of all kinds of things that have been passing through my head in the last year-plus.

I have not been grieving. I did that in 1984 and '5. I cried every night for months and developed clinical depression. That was when I realized that there was no hope of Dick's getting any better than he was at that time, and that the doctors had been either unrealistic or were lying to me. People who have been in any kind of a coma for so long have no chance to escape without brain damage. I have not shed a tear since Dick died. I was very relieved to see him go – he was getting thinner, weaker, older and more confused every day, and I was daily wondering what would happen next.

When I talked to Lois [Spratlen] and told her I had done my grieving years ago, she pressed me to write an article and say just that. She said there are millions of women who have been through that same thing – who do not feel badly when their husbands die. But most of them feel real guilt for not being unhappy at their mates' deaths. She said they all need someone to tell them not to feel guilt. Well, I've just vaguely thought of writing the article so far. I might get to it someday, if there are that many somedays.

I had a good last year at the beach. I am just not good at going places alone yet. And I did do an awful lot of talking to dogs, but that does seem to be dog country out there.

Nellie

We continued to correspond through the 1990s, and visited occasionally. Like Minnie, I continued pursuing my education while working, and I obtained my Master's Degree in Humanities. Greater education and understanding made me more determined to resolve our differences. I felt we only magnified them. She wrote to me:

Dec 1 '94 (What? Already?)

Dear Datter –

It's now 3:15 and neither bed is made. My little mattress has been paining my back so I decided not to make the bed 'till I turned the mattress over – that was yesterday. So I slept in the big bed last night and that's not made either. I'm just goin' all ta hell.

When you were here you said Carl and Starr were far more intellectual than you. That's far from the truth – they are just more knowledgeable about what's goin' on in the world – you're the student; that's what makes one an intellectual. You've been working so hard all your life and going to so many specialized classes (meaning concentrating on one subject) that you haven't done any of the "normal" things that enable one to "chat" and carry on with small talk on the social scene. You'd probably be less miserable if you could do it. What you need to do is fill your head with a lot of different kinds of thoughts so your mind can drift to a lot of different things. That's not putting it very well. Since you haven't begged me to give you any suggestions, of course I want to do it. My little mind at work.

Read "People" magazine once a month.

Read the arts section of the Sacramento Sunday paper twice a month.

Go to a movie twice a month.

Read the front page of your paper; if it is only a weekly you should buy a daily paper and read the front page.

Watch the news on TV as often as possible.

If you don't get any channels on which to watch documentaries, get a "USA Today" and read it all now and then.

Two Sundays a month you could go to church, then to the early Sunday matinee, and get a Sacramento paper on your way home.

Your head would become filled with all kinds of interesting things while you're having a type of recreation.

You'd really begin to feel better. And have things to talk to people about besides work or general miseries.

That's my uncalled-for advice. I love to do this of course, as everyone knows.

I'm doing my Chi Gong as you advised me.

Maybe you could try to think of me as a sort of zany, light-hearted person talking a lot like my mother. I think Minnie was a pretty scary person [to you as a child] as she was always talking very brightly and jollily (is that a word?) to you. I ain't got any mean bones in my head that are perpetually bent on slamming persons. And I'm not a miserable person as I think you and Starr think I am. I've had a lot of fun in my life; probably I can find or see something funny in almost everything.

I know – something else. ("Oh, God, that woman" you're saying.) Buy a magazine you're never read before. You'd have to do that on your Sunday church-movie jaunt where you'll have a choice of magazines. There must be a marvelous magazine-newspaper store in [Sacramento]. We have a terrific one here. I just love to go there and can't believe there are those hundreds of magazines I've never heard of before.

When going to movies look for "Forrest Gump" – it is so good I'd like to go to it every day for at least two weeks in a row.

Okay, I'm quitting for now. Going to toss a chicken thigh into a pot and end up with chicken and noodles.

Love,

"Talks in Riddles"

Her letter caught me off guard. What did I say or write to her to merit this response? I didn't know. As always, tinges of sarcasm and criticism colored her message. I ignored it. I'd already learned many valuable lessons from her – courage, determination and the importance of health. For years, I watched her claim as normal a life as possible while struggling with physical problems. She'd come home from the hospital, feeble and in pain, but still get up and do housework. So weak she could hardly walk, she crawled around her flower garden to tend her plants. She asked me once to drive her to Dick's Tavern, a local hangout, to get cigarettes, so she could sit up late and write even though she was in pain.

When she felt better, she pursued her interests with passion, learning to play guitar (and later giving lessons), becoming a Master Gardener, studying The Course in Miracles, refinishing furniture and becoming a fine cook (finally!). When she was satisfied with her proficiency, she moved on to a new interest. I learned to value my creativity and avidly pursue my interests from her.

I knew who I was by now. I *had* to respond. I wrote:

Dear "Talks,"

Sorry for the delayed reply. All that talking had to sink in. You are right, I am the intellectual, the student, always have been, always will be. I love learning. To me, learning is recreation. I'm not particularly social. I'm definitely not an extrovert. You've been trying to change me into one all my life. Actually, I'm a sensitive introvert; an INFJ if you're familiar with the Myers-Briggs Type Indicator personality assessment. My truth is my own thoughts, emotions, and intuition.

We live in a world of extroverts. They're the people who read all those magazines and newspapers, chat at social hour after church, and stop for lunch on their way to the movies with friends. Sometimes I do feel left out or not accepted, but that is who I am. It would be great to be more social, but I am who I am. I'll never be an extrovert and don't want to be. My truth is valid for me. I like who I am.

I know you mean well. I'm not going to do what you suggest. It's okay for me to be who I am. I am good enough. My God, I'm over fifty and you're still trying to "fix" me. Give it up, Mom!

I believe in a higher power and that I'm guided to learn and do the things that are right for me, for my personal growth and happiness. Yes, I've had a challenging life – it is what it is. It's made me a better person. I accept myself. I make the effort every day to be positive, improve myself, grow spiritually, and love who I am. I think that's enough.

I still love you.

Your daughter

14 ~ Declare to Resolve Grief and Fear Now

I declare I will speak only positive words of faith and victory over myself,
My family, and my future. . . . I will use my words to change my situation.
– Joel Osteen

1990s and beyond – California, Washington, Arizona

I seek solace after Gail's death.

The greater your emotional desire, the more power you feed into the potential. – Dick Sutphen

Gail died in 1998. My reaction was similar to hers after Minnie's death. It was years before I emotionally embraced my loss. For me it was a different loss; not only the loss of a parent, but the loss of what had been absent from the beginning – affection, love, closeness. I was unable to grieve deeply. Intuitively, I sensed my conflict but didn't know how to resolve it.

A new awareness surfaced unexpectedly one evening while sitting at my desk. I was preparing to write my monthly article for our local Master Gardener newsletter. I'd been a Master Gardener for a year and wrote monthly articles as part of my volunteer commitment. I enjoyed it, but had a hard time fitting it into my busy schedule. Again, I'd waited until the last minute to write. As I sat down at my desk, my thoughts wandered. *I am not procrastinating. I've been too busy maintaining this huge yard and working. I can easily get this done tonight and e-mail it tomorrow before I leave for work.* I sighed as my computer booted up. *I'll be up late though to do it. What am I going to write about this month?*

I muddled ideas around in my mind. Herbs. I'd always loved herbs. My first garden as an adult was an herb garden near Silverton, Washington in the national forest northeast of Everett. My husband and I lived there one summer in an old log cabin, once a stage coach waystation, while he worked on fire watch. My thoughts wandered back to Mother. She'd also been a Master Gardener. She grew berries, herbs, vegetables, flowers. She kept pots of herbs on her deck after Dad died and she moved to an apartment. She swore by shallots, parsley and chives. She always had them growing during the summer and fall as well as *Little Finger* miniature carrots and cherry tomatoes.

Mom loved to garden. *Mom loved to garden.* I almost jumped out of my chair. My hands slid off the keyboard into my lap. *We had a common interest after all. And she wrote about gardening – just like I do now. Wow.* It was a lightbulb moment. I sprang up from my desk, and flew into the other room where I'd stashed a small box of family memorabilia in the closet. I hadn't planned look at it until I retired, but I had to see it now. Would there be any clues?

I looked carefully through the box: a packet of her letters, a few old photos, cards she'd sent her grandkids. That was all. Nothing about her writing or gardening. She'd become a Master Gardener in the 1970s. It was now 2011 and she'd passed thirteen years earlier. Guilt over our strained relationship had sulked silently in an unknown abyss in my mind. It now crept into my heart. Why hadn't I recognized our common interest sooner? It might have brought us together. I had no time to research it now, but I was inspired. I sat down and wrote feverishly. I finished my article in an hour and titled it *Mom Said to Plant Shallots.* It was published the following month.

Now I was intrigued. We had more in common than I thought. Our lifelong conflicts had left me uninterested in her. I knew very little of her life. Now I *had* to know. I sensed that new knowledge and understanding could help me feel or even resolve my grief. When I became a Master Gardener, I intuitively knew it would open new doors for me. I had no idea this would be one, nor did I know the magnitude of my quest.

I started researching her life, turning up little. My opportunity for a research trip "home" to Washington State came that summer when I lost my job. I was temporarily free. I put my job search in motion. For the summer, though, I could retrace the phases of her life. I knew nothing about genealogy but I did know how to research. I hadn't spent all those hours at the library in my youth for nothing.

My trip turned up interesting facts, but little about her personally. She was very private, almost to the point of paranoia. Some of her best friends didn't know she wrote articles and short stories. I now faced the proverbial genealogy brick wall. I couldn't crack it now. Mayo notified me I'd been hired, so I ended my trip abruptly and returned home.

With my new job and schedule, I put my search on hold. But my emotional desire had ignited. My mind was actively planning a different tactic to find out what my heart burned to know: who was the real person she'd hidden under the mask of her anxiety, criticism and disagreement? I declared I would unearth the truth and resolve my feelings with forgiveness and love.

Spring 2003 – Riverside, California

What's wrong with my baby?

I do know God is with me in the darkest moments of life. – Don Piper, 90 Minutes in Heaven

Meanwhile, my daughter continued her journey. She'd persevered straight through college and grad school to obtain her Ph.D. in child psychology. She married, worked as a professor and therapist, and had her first child, Luke. Becoming a mother was a thrill for her as she busily balanced her work schedule with caring for the new addition to their family.

Veola shares her story:

I was at work at Biola University, a two-hour drive from home. Carlos, my husband, was a police officer; he was also at work. A call came in with the address of his parents' house which was near ours. His mother was watching Luke, who had gotten sick and had a seizure, so she called 911. Carlos drove there immediately. The EMTs were there and they took Luke to the hospital. Carlos called me. I left work right away. I gripped the steering wheel trying to weave through traffic quickly, honking and cussing at the drivers who were slowing me down. I was stuck on the freeway not knowing what was wrong with my baby, only knowing he was in the hospital. I was shaking; I felt so afraid and stressed to the max.

I finally arrived at the hospital Emergency Room. The doctors couldn't figure out the problem. While we were waiting in a small room by ourselves, Luke had another seizure. I yelled, "Carlos, he's having another seizure!"

Carlos dashed out of the room, found a nurse and gasped, "My son's having a seizure. Can you help us?"

The nurse said "Yes, just a second," and walked away.

He was stunned. He went to the desk to ask another nurse. "My son's having a seizure. Can you help us?"

She said, "Unhuh, just a minute," and started typing on her computer.

He saw a doctor on the phone by the desk. He tapped him on the arm and said, "My son's having a seizure. Can you help us?"

The doctor said, "Unhuh, just a minute."

Carlos rushed back to the room where I was waiting with Luke. My stomach churned as I watched Luke in the midst of the seizure. He'd lost consciousness and his arms and legs were shaking uncontrollably. It seemed like twenty minutes had passed although it had probably been only a few. I looked up as Carlos came in alone. I panicked. "Where's the doctor? Why aren't they coming?"

He threw open the door of the room we were in. He slammed his fist into it with a loud crack and screamed, "Why won't anybody help us? My son's having a seizure!"

Three nurses dashed into the room instantly. "What's going on? How can we help you?"

Carlos was still in uniform, since he'd rushed to the hospital behind the emergency vehicle. Hospital staff panicked at his reaction and called security because he was armed. His Lieutenant came to the hospital to talk to him. When Carlos explained the situation, his Lieutenant reassured him that he probably would have done the same thing.

Luke got a lot of attention from the doctors then. They gave him tests on everything, including a spinal tap. I couldn't even be with him while they did it. I freaked out. They found nothing. Finally they told us to take him home. They gave us a vial of medicine to inject anally, in case he had another seizure – it would stop it immediately.

We were exhausted, emotional, scared. I put Luke in the car seat. We got in the van, and started driving home. I sat in the back to watch him. Suddenly, he started seizing again. I panicked. "Carlos, he's having another seizure, we've got to pull over!"

Carlos pulled over fast, slamming on the brakes. I grabbed Luke from the car seat. Carlos handed me the medicine. I ripped the diaper off and inserted the medicine in his anus. Carlos held him firmly because the gel medicine was leaking out. I suddenly visualized the scene from *The Lion King* where the baby lion was held up before the crowd of animals so they could see their new king. There we stood on the side of the road at midnight, both of us crying, holding our baby up to God and praying, *Okay, God, do whatever you're going to do, because we have no control over this situation.*

The next day, I took him to our pediatrician and explained what had happened. He told Luke to open his mouth, inserted the tongue depressor, and looked at his throat. "He has tonsillitis. It's a common cause of febrile seizures. Around five percent of children get them. He should outgrow it by around age seven."

I was so relieved. It was simple. I could hardly believe the ER staff gave him a battery of tests and never looked at his throat.

He slept with us for several months after that. I laid him on his back and rested my hand on his chest while he slept. I didn't want any more surprises. He had a few more seizures after that and eventually outgrew them – just as our pediatrician predicted.

15 ~ Create Your World with Intention

When you are aware of everything that you are feeling, all the time, you are in continual communication with your soul.
– Gary Zukav

1990s and beyond – California, Washington, Arizona

I continue my healing journey.

Be in tune with yourself and your intentions. That is the key to every positive change.

I had already dealt with my own pressing family issues. My youngest son had become involved with drugs as a young teen. This led to a number of unfortunate actions, which eventually led to long-term institutionalization. I supported and helped him as much as possible, yet I was powerless to change his path. Through my years of therapy, my own inner work and the healing of time, I reconciled much of my grief, guilt and pain. I accepted that I could only control my own life – one of my hardest lessons and one of the toughest for a parent.

I doggedly continued my personal growth. It is said that when the student is ready, the teacher will appear. It worked for me. Each new discipline I explored developed from what had come before, but only once I'd absorbed the previous lesson rationally and emotionally, changed behaviors and felt ready to explore again.

By learning to breathe consciously and fully, we discover and release the core issues now held in our mind and emotions. – Peter Kane

I breathe myself free.

My first breathwork experience was in a class of women. Most were a couple of decades younger than me. I didn't care. I hoped it would help me understand and resolve my childhood issues. Our instructor, Kathleen, had us lie down on the floor in her large, cheerful meeting room, and get comfortable with our blankets and pillows. We had our water bottles and journals handy. She and her assistants walked around the room throughout the session, checking on us, encouraging us to breathe freely. She verbally guided us as we breathed and relaxed deeply. Her mantra: *It's as easy as A, B, C. Just put your Attention on the breath and Breathe until you feel Complete.*

I breathed slowly at first, then faster as we were instructed: in, out, in a circular fashion, smoothly and continuously. I focused on it completely as I sank deeper into relaxation. As if by magic, images came to mind. I was a small child – my mother was scolding me for spilling milk when I fed the kittens . . . we walked through the forest to get the mail . . . tent caterpillars webbed the trees, and sometimes dropped on us – I was afraid. Grandmother Minnie visited us at the tiny house, she tripped and fell . . . I was blamed for not putting the board over the hole to the basement. Time passed . . . I was older, crying in bed because my parents were busy with my baby sister . . . then Mother was sick, I heard her sobbing in pain and feared she would die. The images appeared faster and faster. I started crying uncontrollably. My legs tensed and I drew them up instinctively to fetal position while my hands clenched painfully into fists.

I dimly heard one of the assistants calling me. "Sheryl, just breathe now, calm down. You're okay. Breathe through it; you're almost done."

I breathed deeper. The images disappeared. I relaxed again; my breath slowed. Peace enveloped me.

Afterwards, I sat up abruptly. "I can't believe the images I saw. Those memories were submerged for years." I started writing rapidly in my journal before the intensity of the experience faded. This was a new way to release trauma and pain. It worked.

Breathwork was developed in the 1970s by Leonard Orr, who relived his own birth using a breathing technique he called "rebirthing." This healing practice has since developed and expanded, so "breathwork" is now a more appropriate term. In breathwork, breathing is conscious, full and free. It cleanses the body and emotions, releasing both toxins and trauma.

Focusing on the breath enhances our experience of the present moment. It increases our ability to feel and to be present in our bodies. It heightens both physical and spiritual energy, bringing us to a state where we can relive our birth or re-experience buried trauma and release it permanently. It also invokes our innate spiritual energies, conveying us to a state of bliss.

Breathwork is done under the guidance of a trained breathworker who coaches the client through the breathing process, and provides counseling regarding key emotional issues that arise during the session. Typically, affirmations are developed to support emotional growth. They can be used in many ways. One I've found helpful is to say and write them using first, second and third person ("I create. . . you create. . . Sheryl creates. . ."). This invokes three different mental and emotional pathways to focus and declare my truth. As I repeat or write them, the wording typically transforms to more accurately reflect my needs, underlying feelings and issues.

Through breathwork, I released many traumatic childhood events. I experienced spiritual oneness, serenity, consciousness expansion, and joy. It left me feeling relaxed, peaceful and free. There's a saying in breathwork circles, that if you are horny, hungry and happy after a session, it's been a good one.

All that angry, whiny, petty stuff that you write down in the morning stands between you and your creativity. – Julia Cameron

Journaling accesses my higher wisdom.

I started journaling at twelve. As my writing developed through practice and non-dominant hand techniques, so did my ability to access my inner wisdom. I often jump-start my day with Julia Cameron's "morning pages," three hand-written pages immediately after awakening. This brain dump clears negativity. It allows buried thoughts and emotions to surface, while freeing creativity.

When I first learned to access my inner wisdom using my non-dominant hand to write, intuitive information flowed through me effortlessly from my higher self. I sensed I was being guided. I called this wisdom *SpiritWoman Speaks*. I learned to trust it. I wrote:

> *You have found your path – stay on it and all details will become clear. Time is your ally. Be at peace, go to others with peace.*
>
> *An open throat chakra helps both writing and speaking. It is your responsibility to let others know of your needs.*
>
> *All life is medicine. Medicine for growth; for health, if you allow. Growth does not end; it is process: evolution of infinite possibility. Message for today: allow life to happen. Your goals may be too small. Open the possibility for greater good.*
>
> *The process is what allows you to meet your goal. Process is not linear. It is nature. It is life itself. It convolutes upon itself, creating more possibilities. You are to choose which possibilities you desire. They then change. You cannot control that. You are the actor, but only one actor in process. Movement continues. Process is not standing in the way. It* ***is*** *the way. Enjoy it. It contains infinite possibility.*

Later I affirmed this by writing:

> *I learn to trust my guidance, my body, my feelings. For they alone are true experience for me. I am a microprocessor of experience. I can interpret the data any way I choose. And reinterpret it. Again and again as fits the present instant. I am instamatic. I flash. I video. I tape and replay. And re-film. I allow myself this freedom to change. When I try to stop it, I cause myself pain. When I embrace it, I am fulfilled. I embrace all problems as challenges. I keep them in the present. When I keep problems in the present, I can deal with them as momentary activities. When I chisel them into the future, I cannot. It is then I create my own fear.*

Here is a page of my non-dominant hand journaling, from August 9, 1992:

YOU ASK ABOUT "UNIVERSAL TRUTH."
IT IS YOU. YOU DON'T REALIZE IT.
PHILOSOPHY - LOVE OF WISDOM -
IS NOT INTELLECTUAL, AND IT IS NOT
"ZEN" (USE OF IMMEDIATE KNOWLEDGE.)
IT JUST IS. AND ISN'T. INTELLECT
ALONE CANNOT COMPREHEND, NEITHER
CAN EMOTION ALONE OR INTUITION
ALONE. IT TAKES ALL THREE; A SYNTHESIS!
- AND YOU CAN'T KEEP IT OR STAY IN
THAT PLACE. IT'S "TOUCH AND GO."

IF YOU CAN'T FEEL IT IN YOUR BODY, IT IS
NOT REAL. PHYSICAL FORM IS
NECESSARY FOR ALL EXPERIENCE.
GET IN TOUCH WITH YOUR PHYSICAL
EXPERIENCE OF INTUITION, REASON
AND EMOTION. PAIN AND
PLEASURE ARE YOUR MESSENGER
PIGEONS; THEY ARE YOUR MEANS
OF KNOWING. THEY ARE HOW YOU
KNOW WHERE YOU ARE.

The journal page says:

You ask about "universal truth." It is you. You don't realize it. Philosophy – love of wisdom - is not intellectual. And it is not "Zen" (use of immediate knowledge). It just is. And isn't. Intellect alone cannot comprehend; neither can emotion alone or intuition alone. It takes all three; a synthesis. And you can't keep it or stay in that place. It is "touch and go."

If you can't feel it in your body, it is not real. Physical form is necessary for all experience. Get in touch with your physical experience of intuition, reason and emotion. Pain and pleasure are your messenger pigeons; they are your means of knowing. They are how you know where you are.

I added visual power to journaling with vision boards (treasure maps). They're based on a simple principle – what you visualize or think about consistently, you create in your life. As Shakti Gawain wrote in *Creative Visualization*, "We always attract into our lives whatever we think about the most, believe in most strongly, expect on the deepest levels, and/or imagine most vividly."[34]

I made my first vision board in the early '90s. I'd just read about Sedona, Arizona, with its towering red rock formations and famous energy vortices. I put a small Arizona map on my vision board along with other pictures and affirmations. I visited Sedona four months later.

Vision boards use images and affirmations to strengthen intention and focus. They should resonate with you intuitively. I place affirmations and pictures around my desk, on my whiteboard, and in other areas I use regularly.

This gives me the opportunity to focus on them if only for a moment. We're interrupted many times a day. Much of our time is filled with activities that are "urgent," but not important to the greater ideals of our lives. We must practice with repeated effort to create the lives we desire in accord with our ideals.

I found that mini-vision boards helped me focus on one simple idea and mentally integrate it into my psyche faster. Here's one:

Intention is the highest form of thought.

Healing modalities serve me.

Like Mackie, I found my beliefs and lifestyle the hard way, through the circuitous paths of hardship, poverty, grief, self-doubt and fear. After divorce, I faced the same challenge both Mackie and Minnie had – how to support my family. Through positive thought, prayer and intention, I learned to create my own circumstances consciously, take responsibility and graciously accept help.

Life is change. With free will, we create our reality. The key is discernment. We need to ask ourselves what we want in our lives, and whether we are willing to do the work. The more life-enhancing tools we apply, the more easily we can create positive change or accept unwanted change with a positive attitude, knowing that we can ultimately change that, too.

What we put out, energetically through our emotions and thoughts, and physically through our actions, we receive back. Our interactions mirror our inner selves. This is the law of karma and the principle of the Golden Rule. What we choose, we become.

I learned that to achieve anything, I needed a roadmap of ideals, desires and goals as well as the right tools. I found them by experimentation. I chose to be willing to learn, discover what didn't work, and move on. I practiced what worked for me. In my early intuitive writing, the phrase, "It is your choice," came up many times. I discovered that it's the process that matters. I found if I needed patience, there was always a reason. As came to know myself, I learned to manage and overcome fear. I replaced it with love. That's the ultimate goal.

As a "green," I'm naturally drawn to what is new and educational. Learning is an adventure. I was often ahead of my time, considered foolish or criticized, yet I followed what I felt led to do. Although my temperament seemed like a major negative in my youth, I transformed into the source of my strength.

I realized I had the mental power to create my life. The negative programming I received as a child did not reflect who I was, or who I wanted to be. Every new healing modality added more tools to my toolbox of change. The body-mind is one entity – my studies in Eastern thought and practice taught me that. I incorporated parts of everything I learned into a holistic lifestyle.

Chi Gong, meditation, Reiki, yoga and massage are great energy regulators. I learned and practiced them. I also used exercise and a healthy diet (with lots of veggies from my organic garden) as well as herbs and supplements to improve my health. I continued to "peel the onion" of self and worked through layers of emotional issues using journaling, vision boards, prayer, affirmations and positive imagery.

I spent a year studying with the Science of Mind Church to become a practitioner – a calling similar to that of the Christian Science practitioner, but focused on principles of positive thought rather than the Bible. I didn't complete the course. Instead, other disciplines called me to develop my intuition through deeper meditation, prayer and intuitive writing. Like Mother, I followed my interests to the extent they served me and then pursued something new.

Maybe you are searching among the branches for what only appears in the roots. – Rumi

There are as many tools for positive change as there are temperaments and personality types. Some that worked for me are outlined below. You are unique, and you will find what works for you. Additional information is in Resources.

Affirmations are powerful. I say or chant them aloud while jogging and walking. Recent research shows that physical exercise has extensive and long-lasting influence on cognitive performance (learning, reasoning and problem-solving) and can enhance brain function over a lifetime.[35] Exercise improves both physical fitness and learning power.

I also repeat affirmation keywords as I go to sleep and awaken, when I'm in the alpha state, or periodically during the day. (This is Joseph Murphy's Baudoin technique.)[36] It becomes a mantra that cues the mind and functions as a subconscious context for the day's thoughts.

I found that it's effective to read affirmations and goals while looking in a mirror. This typically brings up emotional resistance (*I don't deserve that* or *I'm not good enough*). These feelings can be overcome with patience, repetition and time. When we experience them, they dissipate into neutrality.

Mind Mapping uses a visual, creative and colorful diagram that's useful for organizing information. It's usually created around a single concept, which is shown in the center of the page, with corollary ideas, words and images branching out from it so all parts are interrelated. It's helpful for clarifying goals and solving problems.

Self-hypnosis has unlimited possibilities. In a state of deep relaxation, I've changed habits and attitudes, and focused on attaining goals. I use my own script, read affirmations aloud quietly or repeat them silently. I've also taped my script and listened to my voice, which is probably most effective. *Instant Self-Hypnosis* by Forbes Robbins Blair gives many sample scripts that can be personalized.

Prayer has always been a part of my spiritual practice. Writing gratitude statements as a form of prayer lifts my spirit. I pray for centering, protection, and clear access to higher consciousness before meditating. I also use an affirmative method of prayer based on faith. "You must ask *believing*, if you are to receive."[37]

In *The Science of Mind*, Ernest Holmes explains a powerful five-part affirmative prayer process. It is simple: acknowledge God or the Source, affirm your oneness with God, positively state your desired condition or result, give thanks, and finally, release the prayer to God.[38]

I started meditating at thirteen and have practiced many forms. I now study Chan (Chinese Zen) with a group led by Gilbert M. Gutierrez, in Riverside, California. He is one of five lay Dharma heirs of Venerable Chan Master Sheng Yen, who founded Dharma Drum Mountain meditation and learning centers in Taiwan and New York State. Gilbert's lectures and discussions always inspire me to think, question, and awaken to greater illumination. Access to his Dharma talks is available on line via podcast or email subscription. In one lecture, Gilbert said:

> *There's nothing hard to the practice of Chan. You just have to put the mind in the present moment and see what is arising moment to moment, understanding that all phenomena that are arising are connected in some way or another. All phenomena are coming up because of causes and conditions – the causes from before will bring forth certain conditions now, and those conditions will turn to causes for future conditions. When we see things in this*

way, we're clear about what's happening. We're not seeing things from a viewpoint of escaping blame for whatever we've done, or ignoring how mind works.[39]

Feng Shui, literally translated, is "wind" and "water." It is the harmonious arrangement of our surroundings to enhance the flow of chi to balance Yin and Yang. When I first studied Feng Shui, I rearranged my house to attract money. Within a week, a friend repaid a debt of $500.00. Feng Shui teaches us to balance the energies of our environment; it balances us in the process.

Reiki harnesses universal life force energy, which is channeled through chakras (energy centers) in the palms of the hands. You must be initiated into Reiki by a Reiki master. Once your energy imprint is changed with Reiki, you will always have it. Reiki induces a deeply relaxed state, balances energy, and facilitates healing of emotional and physical issues.

Chi Gong is the art of personal energy manipulation through movement and breath. It balances energy while increasing the flow of chi, which enlivens the body, improves health, and prolongs life. There are many forms of Chi Gong which use different types of practice. Universal Chi Gong, which I studied, combines different styles for health and vitality.

Mudras (symbolic hand gestures, movements or poses) are another way to focus energy and attention on specific chakras to strengthen them and enhance the flow of chi. They can be used alone or as part of a meditation or yoga practice. The hand postures are simple, can be held for as little as three minutes, and produce powerful effects on both physical and spiritual energy.

The Bible – the supreme guide to fulfillment

Veola sought her faith in Christianity, Bible study and the companionship of like-minded Christians. She followed a more traditional path than I did in finding God, herself and her faith. Her devotional below encourages us to seek in the true Christian way: to fulfill our needs through God, our source.

Veola shares this devotional:

Are You Thirsty?

Blessed are those who hunger and thirst for righteousness, for they will be filled. – Matthew 5:6

In the *Rime of the Ancient Mariner*, Coleridge wrote, "Water, water everywhere, nor any drop to drink."

That was the situation for 900 sailors floating in the ocean after an attack on their ship during World War II. Of the 900 men who survived the attack, rescuers found only 316. Sadly, many of the men died in the water because they chose to drink it.

The salinity of seawater makes a person sick. These sailors knew it. They also knew that if they ingested enough, it would cause hallucinations, paranoia and eventually death. Despite being aware of these possibilities, many of the sailors drank anyway. Their thirst made them search for anything that would quench it.

I often feel like one of these sailors – thirsty, tired and needy. Yet, I search for relief in the wrong way. I watch television; I keep too busy or eat too much to find contentment. It's no surprise, I'm still thirsty. The satisfaction I seek feels elusive and unattainable.

There is only one way to satisfy a dry soul: through the One who calls Himself the "Living Water." The Lord promises to fulfill all our needs. The requirement? Come to Him. When we do, we'll no longer feel like a sailor floating in undrinkable water.

So, are you thirsty today? How will you quench your thirst?[40]

16 ~ Finding Faith and Creating Understanding

I know when God sees my faith, He will show up and do amazing things.
– Joel Osteen

2009 – Riverside, California

Is Luke's naïve faith enough?

You have the wisdom within you.

In quenching our thirst with God, we can learn from children who find it easy to turn to Him for answers. Their faith is innocent, open, believing. Veola's nine-year old went directly to God for help when he had a crisis. She shares his story:

On a chilly Saturday morning in mid-March I chatted with a friend as we settled in to watch her twins play baseball. My son, Mark, played in the grass nearby, occasionally sneaking a peek to check on his friends' accomplishments. Midway through the fourth inning, my cell phone buzzed. My husband's name appeared on the screen. "Hey, honey, what's up?" I said.

"Something terrible happened," Carlos said between jagged breaths.

I couldn't swallow when I heard his tone. My deepest fears played in my imagination. Was our oldest son in the hospital? Had a family member been in a car accident?

"It's Paco. He's alive – but I don't . . . think . . . he's going to make it," he told me in broken sentences.

Luke, our nine-year old son, had been playing in his room with our miniature Dachshund, Paco, while he waited for a friend to pick him up for a playdate. Carlos, enjoying the quiet of the morning, rested on the couch with a wheelchair nearly. A broken leg and recent surgery on his rotator cuff had left him nearly immobile.

With idle time and a dog at his side, Luke grabbed a few toy cars and zoomed them across his wooden bedroom floor. He took a look out of his window. As was normal for a Saturday morning, the neighbor's grandmother lounged on their porch. She waved to Luke.

With a smile, Luke greeted her and opened the window. Her grandchildren joined her, excited to "talk" with Luke. Despite being within earshot, usually no one spoke. Luke was accustomed to pantomiming to the family due to the grandmother's limited English.

As he made faces and gestures at the group, a thought occurred to Luke. He dropped to the ground and grabbed Paco. Surely a wiener dog would make anyone smile. He propped Paco against the screen and pretended to make the dog wave. Just as he did so, Paco leaned further forward. Thinking the mesh would hold the dog's weight, Luke loosened his grip. Paco fell two stories and landed on the concrete patio below.

Witnessing Paco's fall, the children and grandmother screamed. Luke held his breath. He leaned over the window's edge to see Paco splayed out on the concrete, not moving. Luke ran down the stairs, taking them two at a time.

"Dad! Dad! Paco fell!"

Carlos rubbed his eyes. "Huh?"

Luke skidded to a stop in front of the couch. "It's Paco, he fell out my window. He's by the trailer."

Carlos jumped up, ready to search for the dog, but the pain in his leg stopped him. He moved toward the wheelchair but realized it would not fit through the narrow RV parking area. Carlos, undeterred, eyed the spot where he usually left his crutches. Not finding them, he took a deep breath and started toward the trailer, one hop at a time, in pain.

He found Paco on the ground in the middle of a seizure. Shaken by the dog's appearance, he picked him up gently and considered his options while Luke looked on, witnessing Paco's suffering. He hobbled back inside the house and wrapped the seizing dog in a blanket. He knew he had to get the dog to the vet right away. First he called me. Being over an hour away from home at the baseball game, I couldn't offer immediate help. His next choice was to call the family of the friend Luke had been waiting for. No answer. He looked down at Paco, still in his arms, now shivering. He placed the dog on the ground next to the fireplace where he had a small flame burning and tried the friend again, getting no response.

Carlos turned to Luke, wanting to reassure him. "When they get here, we'll ask them to take us." He then smoothed his hand over Paco's fur and whispered to comfort the dog. "It will be alright, Paco. You're okay."

Luke studied Paco. He appeared grotesque. Eyes rolled back, foaming at the mouth and immobile, he seemed ready to die. "I can't handle seeing him like this," Luke said and ran back to his room. Luke covered his head with his comforter and buried himself under a pile of pillows. "Please, Lord, don't take my dog from me," he begged. "We're not done having adventures together. He's my best friend." He continued in prayer this way, head hidden and heart lifted to the Lord for half an hour.

As Luke continued to pray, and Carlos whispered love into the dog's ear, our friends tapped the doorbell. It rang throughout the house. Paco leaped from his blankets near the fire and sprinted to the door. He barked and growled as was his typical response to the doorbell. Carlos's hand stood frozen over the spot where he had been petting the dog. Luke flew out of his room. "What happened? Is Paco okay?"

Carlos shuffled to the door. He found Luke staring at Paco, confused by his sudden recovery. Now jumping and scratching at the door, the dog appeared completely normal. Carlos and Luke looked at each other with uncertainty and the bell chimed again.

With a slight nudge to get Paco away from the door, Carlos let our visitors in. He explained what had happened and his desire to take Paco to the vet. Yet, when he looked at Paco jumping up on Luke's friend, it seemed he didn't need medical attention. More than that, he seemed unusually healthy.

Carlos set the dog on the couch, running his hand along every part of his body, looking for areas where he might wince in pain. Nothing came of it. The dog panted and rubbed himself into Carlos' hand longing for another caress. He didn't wince, yelp or act in any way as if he were injured.

"Seems fine to me," our friend said.

Without question, Luke understood. "I prayed," he told Carlos. "God healed him." Luke, certain of God's intervention, thanked the Father, gave Paco a hug and left within minutes for his playdate, appearing to be without a worry. God had caused the trauma of the morning to pass. Luke didn't look back. Paco never again showed evidence of having fallen out of the window.

1990s – California

I re-experience my birth.

Every emotion is part of ego and needs to be fully experienced to be released.

Long before I had children, I vowed to parent differently from my mother. I was painfully aware of the injury I'd sustained from her prohibitive standards and unending criticism. However, as I matured, I realized how similar we were. I pledged to focus on the positive things I'd learned from her: determination, courage, independence, humor, the power of thought, creativity . . . faith.

Like all parents, I had to start where I was. With no parenting skills or knowledge of child psychology, I matured emotionally with my family. Therapy, parenting groups, school counselors and personal growth helped me develop new, positive parenting skills. Could I finally overcome all the negativity, fear and criticism I'd learned as a child? I searched for more answers in a breathwork session.

At our meeting room, I gazed out of the long windows overlooking new-growth forest shrouded peacefully in mist. I positioned myself on the purple yoga mat, put a pillow under my knees, pulled the blanket snugly up to my neck to minimize body-temperature changes, and closed my eyes. I breathed deeply and quickly.

I was experienced at breathwork now. Eva, my coach for this session, sat on the floor beside me. As breathwork partners, we took turns being the coach and the subject. She encouraged me, "That's a good start, keep it up, you're doing fine."

I focus totally on the present moment. Time disappears as I breathe deeper. Air flows through my lungs, heart, chest and head, then down through my abdomen, legs and feet. I ride on the crest of the breath in a sea of expanding energy.

"Good job. Keep going; a little faster now."

I breathe faster, deeper. I sense tetanus – involuntary muscle convulsions in my hands. I breathe through it and it disappears. I'm in a deeper state now. I float on the breath peacefully. Suddenly, I feel squeezed all over. I can't move. My breath sticks in my throat. I choke and panic.

"Relax, now. Breathe yourself through it. You can do it."

I hear Eva's reassuring voice as if it were far away. Suddenly I convulse, the lower part of my body twisting, writhing. Tension envelops my abdomen. My legs tremble with the sensation of pins and needles. My core feels rigid, my mind anxious.

I realize I am experiencing myself as a fetus in the womb. I sense something noxious, feel tension in my stomach. I'm uneasy. I immediately feel pressure and release as if I were moving. Almost as quickly my head feels free; my body relaxes. But I choke, unable to breathe. Tightness envelops my neck. It lasts for a moment, then releases.

On the yoga mat, I sigh, relax and release a long slow breath. My energy expands. Golden light fills my energy field. Deeply peaceful, in a meditative state, I rest, allowing the energy to flow where it will, and envelop me with light, peace, love. Gradually I regain full awareness, sit up and drink water. I have just re-experienced my birth.

Eva hugs me. "Great job. You went very deep today. You breathed yourself through it."

"Thank you." I hug her back, glad to be done and grateful for my experience. I open my notebook and begin to write.

> *I wanted to be born. The womb was toxic for me. My mother smoked while she was pregnant. I sensed her anxiety about the pregnancy and my birth. I needed to leave an unhealthy environment. Could this be why I was born early? She told me once that the umbilical cord was wound around my neck at birth. That may explain why I couldn't wear turtleneck shirts; I felt choked. My birth makes sense to me now. Through this experience I can*

embrace a fresh understanding of my childhood sensitivities and stomach issues. I was stressed even before birth.

My affirmations were:

It's safe to be here.

I am welcome in the world.

It's good to be alive.

I'm good enough as a woman.

17 ~ Reaching Your Bliss

Follow your bliss and the universe will open doors where there were only walls. – Joseph Campbell

The Light is *in* you. – A Course in Miracles

Present time to eternity

We are all an expression of God.

The same law of light reigns for the unseen shining as for the manifest. – Emma Curtis Hopkins, High Mysticism

I imagine Mackie sitting in her parlor after church in the big, comfortable foursquare house on NW 56th Street in Ballard, talking with Mary, her friend from their Grays Harbor days. Golden loaves of freshly baked bread adorn the kitchen counter. A pot of hot tea rests on the cozy on the parlor table as the two friends relax. Mackie's wearing her favorite purple taffeta dress. Her wide-brimmed straw hat rests on the sofa nearby. Her short, curly hair is pushed back from her face.

"Thanks for inviting me over today." Mary gave Mackie a big hug.

"You're welcome." Mackie motioned to the teapot. "Help yourself."

"Thank you." Mary reached for the teapot and poured herself a cup of tea.

Mackie settled into her chair. "It's so good to sit and visit again. We haven't seen each other since church a couple of months ago. Did John find a job?"

Mary nodded. "Yes. He went to work in one of the new retail shops on Market Street. He loves it; it's always busy and he can visit with the customers. It suits his outgoing personality. I'm so relieved. Mackie, you were right. I prayed about it and everything worked out for the best. An acquaintance offered him a job not long after we talked."

Mackie smiled. "That's wonderful. My sixth sense told me that someone would help you very soon."

"I'm grateful." Mary paused and pursed her lips. A slight frown crossed her face. She stretched out her leg and showed Mackie her swollen ankle. Her long maroon skirt brushed the top of it. "Now I have other worries. Look at this. I fell and twisted my ankle. I stayed off my feet for a couple of days, elevated and iced it, but it's still swollen and bruised. I can walk of course, but it's not healing properly. I've prayed about it, too. I'm worried."

"Let's see what *Science and Health* says." Mackie picked it up off the table and read aloud: " 'Man is an expression of God's being.' " She set the book down and looked at Mary. "You know, if this is true, we can manifest nothing unlike God. We are God's reflection. God is infinite and there is no other power. When we have more faith in God than we do in ourselves, no material belief can prevent us from healing the sick."[41]

Mary sat back in her chair. Her lips parted and she let out a long breath.

"I truly believe that. Sometimes I just feel that my prayers aren't strong enough; that I'm not strong enough."

Mackie smiled. "I understand. Reading and studying makes our faith stronger. I saw an article in *The Christian Science Journal* that expresses the same thing." She picked up the magazine and read: " 'Man has never been anything but the expression of God. . . . Since nothing unlike God can enter his being, we can rest in sweet assurance that nothing unlike Him can enter His manifestation.' "[42]

"That's so inspiring. I only need to know and believe that my ankle is a perfect expression of God and is healed."

"Yes, you can only be in perfect health. You need to know it, feel it, believe it. She picked up *Science and Health* again, turned the pages, and read: " 'The Divine Principle, or Spirit, comprehends and expresses all, and all must therefore be as perfect as the divine Principle is perfect.' "[43]

Mackie placed the book gently on the table. She smiled her huge smile. Her whole aura glowed. She exuded love, confidence and joy. "I really love this. I feel closer to God just by reading it, and I sense God's healing power generating within me."

Mary leaned closer to Mackie, gazing at her intently. "I know in my heart this is true. I will pray about it again."

Mackie reassured her, "You are in perfect health now. Believe it because that *is* your true self. It can't be otherwise."

"I understand. I can't have a mental condition other than that of God, so I can't be injured or ill. That's inconsistent with God's being as well as my own."

"Of course. Mrs. Eddy said that matter has no consciousness or ego. Its conditions are illusory and the source of sickness. When fear is gone, so is the foundation of disease."[44]

"I need to be more confident in God."

Mackie said, "God is accessible to all. Nothing is too hard for God, or for us if we harness the power of God. We need to be open to spirit and ready to accept our good. It can give us only what we can accept. Prayer should be our active acceptance of His highest willingness. It must be constructive."

Mary's eyes brightened and her lips parted. "I understand. Jesus said: *It shall be done to you according to your faith.* I am ready to pray. I feel better already." She bowed her head and closed her eyes. She relaxed into the chair and took a deep breath. She murmured, "I am ready to heal. I feel God's power working through me now."

Mackie also bowed her head and prayed silently. *Let the healing power of Jesus be with us now. We are open to Your will.* She spoke: "There is no other existence but spiritual existence. As we have learned, and you have taught us Lord, mind alone possesses all perception and comprehension. Our nature is identical to yours. We possess the same inherent attributes as from where we came. We contain the ocean of our creator within us. We know that right where the pain appears to be, the presence of God is. In this presence there is no strife. Only peace and ease remain. Thank you, Lord, for this healing."

Mary opened her eyes and blinked. Sunlight flowed in through the lace curtains, bathing the room in a soft light. "I feel much better now.

My pain is gone. I feel lighter in spirit too, more at peace, knowing I am healthy and whole. Thank you so much, Mackie."

"You're welcome. Prayer is a blessing. Just hold the right thought and pray. We can heal as Jesus did. God will lead you to greater understanding of the truth."

"Thank you. I really love talking with you. I always go home feeling so much better. I feel peaceful now, hopeful too. My ankle pain is gone. I'm encouraged by your understanding and faith. I still don't know how you do it; your life's been so challenging."

"Oh, it's based on love, that's all. I've always believed it's better to do for others – better for the spirit. I'm happy to help others because of the healing I've experienced. I knew in my heart that I could help others heal as I had healed. God works through me just as He works through all of us. God produces the healing through our intention, emotion and love. Our thoughts are not just things; they are the cause of things. It's a blessing that I'm able to transfer my passion and joy about my faith in God to others, through love. I don't know how it works – it just does."

"I am blessed. I've taken our prayers directly into my heart. I can pray now with feeling and gratitude for the healing. You are such an inspiration to me, Mackie."

"I'm so glad." Her warm smile brightened her whole face and spread love through the room. She laughed, reached across the table and squeezed Mary's hand. "Remember now, we're just talking."

Is God your Wonderful Counselor?

God has no office hours. There is never a time when God is unavailable. – Emmet Fox

Carrying the energy of faith and healing forward in a modern setting, Veola encourages us see God as our "wonderful counselor" who should be the backbone of all our plans.

James 1:5 – "If any of you lacks wisdom, you should ask God, who gives generously to all without finding fault, and it will be given to you."

Everyone has a consultant today. Small businesses seek help with taxes. Therapists ask other counselors for guidance. Even churches bring in outside people to strategize about goals.

On a personal level, I love to "consult" with friends about how to handle a sticky situation. After a long chat, I feel as if I've found the answers to life's problems. The truth is, I now have one more problem – I've left God out of my "consultation." I come up with a quick fix instead of depending upon Him. Have you done the same?

We hurt ourselves and grieve the spirit of God when we leave Him out of our plans and problems. He is much more than just another consultant. He is our "Wonderful Counselor." Who is He to you?[45]

Ascension into the Light

Travel light, live light, spread the light, be the light. – Yogi Bajan

Connection with spirit and the energy of unconditional love were the basis of my healing modalities and all I'd learned. In a breathwork session, I attained a state of peace within, transcending all physical and emotional symptoms. I simply went into the gap between thoughts that Deepak Chopra speaks of. I felt the presence of God, the Divine.

My breathwork coach covered me with a thick blanket as I lay on the massage table. She turned on quiet, New Age music, put lavender oil in the diffuser and lit the candle. I settled serenely into relaxation.

The soothing scent of lavender oil wafted into my nostrils. I relaxed into comfort and well-being. The soft background music resonated with electronic chords, muted chanting and a coyote's solitary wail. It gave me a sense of otherworldly stillness. My breath flowed easily.

I relaxed deeply and quickly. I felt the presence of divine love surround me. I was immersed in swirling light; magenta flowed into teal, then yellow transformed to blue. It flowed into my crown chakra at the top of my head and down through my body. I felt the presence of subtle vibrations, the creative force, universal energy. Bliss enveloped every breath, pore and fiber of my being. Images floated effortlessly before my inner eye. I visualized myself as an otherworldly warrior of the light, healed in spirit, emanating healing energy and unconditional love from the source. It was mystical. I was one with the Light.

Afterwards, I wrote my experience in my journal. My higher guidance spoke through me as Lahoun, which is my spiritual name:

I am Lahoun, Goddess of the Holy Order of the Light, and this ring is my seal.

I bring the message of light to Earth.

I breathe in liquid light that dances on the sea. I illumine the Earth and empower it with light energy for all.

Throughout the universe, all is light – the essence of creation; the luminosity of pure being.

We are all beings of light; part of that glow which radiates throughout the universe, emanating from our hearts through love, from our minds with true knowing and from our bodies as pure energy.

We are the energy potential filling the Earth with love, knowledge, wisdom and joy.

We are aligned with the light when balanced in body and spirit.

As we refine our bodies and hearts with well-being, compassion and love, we impart it to others and bring them into the light also.

Our innermost being is of the light. Our hearts light our earthly bodies. As we expand our heart-lights to encompass others, love and understanding enlarge exponentially, transmuting all.

We each bring our message of illumination to earth in our own unique and perfect way.

The light of knowledge in each soul is an ember, emanating from the source. As we awaken, it brightens and we grow with forgiveness and understanding.

Our expanded light beams to others, lifting their burden and enlightening the Earth.

In the light of love we are one. As we give to others, we bring ourselves into the light. Love is in every heart; let it shine to heal the world.

Even the breath is of the light. Through our breath, we transform light into cellular energy. We breathe light into our bodies and span the cosmos with our brilliance.

In our deepest beings we transform our radiance into bliss, enlightening others as well as ourselves.

As we raise our vibration, we transcend duality; we are one with each other and the source. All is one.

So call forth your inner light, your unique luminescence, and shine it upon the world with your own special glow.

Be the bliss you truly are. Share your unique gift – your light – with the world, and illuminate it.

Move forth through faith, empower yourself and assist others to transcend into joy.

Faith, power and joy magnetize us to illumination.

Our home is forever in the Light.

Epilogue

The only journey is the one within. – Rainer Maria Rilke

I started researching this book in the summer of 2011. My research trip to Washington that summer was geared to learning about my mother. I felt that new information would help me understand her differently and help heal the remaining grief I'd put on ice for so long. I also wanted to write about her and celebrate her life.

During my research process, I recognized that she was a product of her family – one I didn't know. Our family wasn't close. Although I couldn't change that dynamic, I could offer a fresh perspective. I had no idea that the research process, as well as my own thoughts and feelings, would spark my personal and spiritual growth. I had begun a mysterious inner journey.

My life expanded with growth and change. After returning from my first research trip, I started another day job with the same wonderful group of scientists I'd worked with previously. I worked three more years and retired for my third time. I took two more research trips, survived rotator-cuff surgery on my right shoulder (I'm right-handed), continued volunteering as a Master Gardener and became an herbalist. I maintained a 10,000 square-foot property teeming with plant life, wrote lots of articles on gardening, ended a long-term relationship and moved to a new residence.

Those changes involved the physical world. As overwhelming as they were, my personal growth outpaced them. My emotional and spiritual evolution escalated. I began to feel even more strongly that I was spiritually called to write this book. But what had I really committed to? Could I finish it and did I even know where it was leading me? I realized this was the most significant project I'd ever undertaken. It involved knowing and accepting myself and my family on a completely different spiritual level. I felt I was navigating a sacred path begun by my foremothers.

During the writing process, I often thought I could wrap the whole project up right away. Then I realized I had more work to do on myself. I hadn't fully resolved the issues that my research and memories had uncovered. I needed to be complete, and feel neutral about it. Meditation, intuitive writing and rewriting became my method.

The writing itself challenged me. I love non-fiction because I love to learn. I was determined to write a non-fiction book and confident I'd find all the information. I was naive and wrong. As I delved deeper into genealogy, my curiosity increased and my research expanded. After learning about the three generations before me, I wrote a series of essays about the women, thinking it would be the basis for my book. That was book number one.

As I meditated, I became more receptive. Afterward, intuitive information about my ancestors flowed into my mind. I wrote quickly as the surge increased and my inner author flourished. The more I allowed this stream-of-consciousness wisdom to flow through me, the better at it I became. Ultimately, I ended up with binders full of intuitive writing. That became the second book.

Then I discovered Tom Bird. I attended his introductory lecture on writing. In a writing exercise, he led us into a deeply relaxed state where we could contact our internal author and write rapidly to maintain the intuitive flow. His method was similar to my own. I signed up for his upcoming weekend workshop. Using his method, I completed my book in a long weekend. So now I had three books.

By that time, I'd progressed into my fifth year of research and writing. I attended two more writing workshops, revised the previous books, and started another. I put it on the shelf with no revisions. Where was this going to end?

The first book encapsulated my research. It created the factual basis for my soul's understanding of the family. The second book generated a spiritual synopsis of the family as a whole. It included my perception of the life paths each chose, what we were here to accomplish or learn, and how these interactions furthered our own personal and spiritual growth, as well as that of the family.

The third book fostered my own spiritual growth. I realized why I was so passionate about sharing what I'd learned. These women and our intergenerational connection galvanized me. I was continuing the spiritual path they'd started. Their lives were inspirational. I wanted to portray their distinctive qualities: faith, compassion, love, determination and courage. I yearned to celebrate the family similarities and minimize the differences.

I labored to combine the three books, weaving the women's stories through periods of time, personal life situations and their unique personalities. I layered the emotion with factual information and their life lessons. Their faith, power and joy soared from the page.

I couldn't have written this book any sooner or faster. I coped with my emotions, re-experiencing issues I thought were resolved, but which had resurfaced. I struggled to fathom the depth of my feelings and reach a new viewpoint. My understanding had to mature. That took time, and working through my own issues again.

I recognized we are here to support each other in our roles and understand ourselves in relationship to our family members. Mutual support and understanding are vital aspects of family. Each unique individual plays a significant role; a part no one else can play in the family dynamic. We are here to comprehend and embrace our differences, relish our uniqueness and accept our shadow selves. We are here to turn the dark into light, anger to forgiveness and differences into understanding.

Eventually, I completed my task. I found my book. I incorporated the best of my three books into one. I am grateful for the journey. I hope my family's lessons and personal growth will inspire you to understand yourself, embrace your family, and transform differences into harmony. We are here to revive our faith, wield our power for the highest good, and bestow joy. In the end, we can all become bringers of the light.

Notes

1. "223 Are Graduated from Tacoma High," *The Daily Ledger*, June 14, 1912.

2. "Freshman Class History." *Whitworth College Bulletin* (1914), 40.

3. "Everett Massacre (1916)," Margaret Riddle. Essay 9981. Posted December 18, 2011. http://www.historylink.org/File/9981.

4. *The Wayfarer*, University of Washington Library, Special Collections, Accession Name: The Wayfarer, Accession Number 4715-001, Folder Number VF #326.

5. *The Wayfarer*, University of Washington Library, Special Collections, Accession Name: Meisnest, Darwin; Accession Number 2945-81-41, Box No. 1, Folder Number: Wayfarer.

6. "Everett Massacre (1916)."

7. *The Ocean Breeze* (Volume XIX, Number 16, Weatherwax High School, Aberdeen, Washington, Wednesday, April 28, 1926): 3.

8. Mary Baker Eddy, *Science and Health with Key to the Scriptures*, 1875. (Boston: First Church of Christ, Scientist, 1934) 1:1-3.

9. Eddy, *Science and Health*, 468:12-15, 248:26-29.

10. *Quinault Yearbook*, Weatherwax High School, 1926, p. 67.

11. Louis Beach, *The Goose Hangs High, A Play in Three Acts* (Boston: Little, Brown and Company, 1926), 150.

12. Bible Lesson Sermon, *Substance*, Sunday, September 12, 1926. *Science and Health with Key to the Scriptures*, Mary Baker Eddy, Section I (1) 335:12 and (2) 349:31.

13. Eddy, *Science and Health*, 468:18-19.

14. "Fluoxetine." Wikipedia. https://en.wikipedia.org/wiki/Fluoxetine.

15. Peter B. Biggins, "Divine Love's Provision," *Christian Science Sentinel,* Vol. XXIX, No. 4 (September 25, 1926): 63.

16. The "other person" Gail knew who possessed remarkable charisma was Ben K. Weatherwax, a cherished family friend. He was an outstanding dramatics student of Minnie's who came from a Grays Harbor pioneer family. After high school, he attended college and entered the broadcasting industry. He married Marian Abel and had two children. Ben served in WWII and was a Marine Corps major when discharged. He returned to Grays Harbor, started radio station KBKW, and was a well-known radio commentator. His program, "Hometown Scrapbook," celebrated the local lives and diversity of Grays Harbor. He was also an artist, architect and contractor. "The Entrance" (p. 38) is one of his high school drawings for the 1927 *Quinault,* the Weatherwax High School Yearbook. Ben died tragically in a fire at his beach home in 1956. He was forty-seven.

17. John C. Hughes and Ryan Teague Beckwith, Eds. *On the Harbor, From Black Friday to Nirvana*, (Aberdeen: The Daily World, 2001), 2.

18. "Buy on Grays Harbor." *The Aberdeen Daily World*, (March 9, 1934): 12.

19. Minnie Moore McDowell, *Shakespeare's Likeness to Castiglione: an Indication of Probable Indebtedness* (University of Washington, 1935): 111.

20. *Fashionable Dress Individual Horoscope of Gail Klingberg.* Cast by Polly Patterson.

21. "We Celebrate at Tryout." *Tryout Times* (Vol. 1, No. 2, October 1944): 2-3. University of Washington Library, Special Collections, Accession Name: George M. Savage Papers, Accession Number 5400-001, Box Number 21, Folder Number 6.

22. "Who's Who in Tryout – Record of First Year." *Tryout Times* (Vol. 1, No. 2, October 1944): 3. Her articles were published in the following publications: *Variety, Players Magazine, Virginia Drama News, National Theatre Conference Bulletin, Cameo* and *Broadsides.* University of Washington Library, Special Collections, Accession Name: George M. Savage Papers, Accession Number 5400-001, Box Number 21, Folder Number 6.

23. Minnie Moore McDowell, "Tryout Theatre," *Cameo*, Zeta Phi Eta (May 1944): 36.

24. Minnie Moore McDowell, "Play Surgery at Tryout Theatre," *Virginia Drama News* (Vol. XII, No. 8, 15 May 1944): 2-3.

25. Lucia Capacchione, *The Power of Your Other Hand: A Course in Channeling the Inner Wisdom of the Right Brain*, rev. ed., (Pompton Plains: New Page/The Career Press, 2001), 112.

26. John Bradshaw, *Healing the Shame that Binds You.* (Deerfield Beach: Health Communications, 1988), 10.

27. Capacchione, *The Power of Your Other Hand,* 16.

28. Joseph Murphy, Ph.D., D.D., *The power of Your Subconscious Mind.* Edited and revised by Arthur R. Pell, Ph.D. (New York: Prentice Hall, 2008), 85-87.

29. *Real Colors Summary*, Mayo Foundation for Medical Education and Research, Human Resources Education and Development, 2009.

30. Real Colors Workshop, Mayo Clinic, Scottsdale, AZ, 2014.

31. "Are You Stagnant or Growing?" Bible Study Blog. veolavazquez.com.

32. https://www.silvamethod.com

33. Joseph Murphy, 88, 90.

34. Shakti Gawain, *Creative Visualization: Use the Power of Your Imagination to Create What You Want in Your Life*. rev. ed. (Novato: New World Library, 2002): 11.

35. Scientific American, *How Does Exercise Benefit Cognition?* David R. Jacobs, Ph.D. and Na Zhu. https://www.scientificamerican.com/article/how-does-exercise-benefit-cognition/

36. Joseph Murphy, 85-6.

37. Joseph Murphy, 82.

38. Ernest Holmes, *The Science of Mind: A Philosophy, A Faith, A Way of Life* (New York: Tarcher/Putnam, 1966), 149-176.

39. Gilbert Gutierrez, Dharma Talk, October 17, 2016, Riverside, CA.

40. "Are You Thirsty? Finding Contentment and Satisfaction." Bible Study Blog. veolavazquez.com.

41. Eddy, *Science and Health,* 470:23-24; 471:17-19; 368:15-17.

42. E. Violet J. Dicksee, "God Is All." *The Christian Science Journal,* Vol. 46, No. 3 (June 1928): 135.

43. Eddy, *Science and Health,* 518:27-29.

44. Eddy, Science and Health, 368:24-32.

45. "Is God Your Wonderful Counselor?" Bible Study Blog. veolavazquez.com.

Resources

Here are some resources for holistic wellbeing, spirituality, personal growth and empowerment. Many are mentioned in the text; others I've found equally helpful. Some are classics in spiritual and psychological growth traditions. Many of the authors have additional books, websites, blogs, newsletters and videos. A brief list of on-line and other resources is also included.

Books

Abbott, David. W. *Scenario Role Play: The Blees Method.* Author House, 2005.

A Course In Miracles, Foundation for Inner Peace, 1975, 1985.

Arrien, Angeles. *The Second Half of Life: Opening the Eight Gates of Wisdom.* Sounds True, 2007.

A Search for God, Books I and II. Compiled by Study Group #1, Association for Research and Enlightenment. 1942, 1970.

Baker, Irina. *Keys to Freedom: The Guide to Personal Power.* Irina Baker, 2009.

Beattie, Melody. *Codependent No More: How to Stop Controlling Others and Start Caring for Yourself.* The Hazelden Foundation, HarperCollins, 1987.

Bernstein, Gabrielle. *The Universe Has Your Back: Transform Fear to Faith.* Hay House, Inc. 2016.

Blair, Forbes Robbins. *Instant Self-Hypnosis: How to Hypnotize Yourself with Your Eyes Open.* Sourcebooks, Inc., 2004.

Bradshaw, John. *Healing the Shame that Binds You.* Health Communications, Inc., 1988.

—. *Homecoming: Reclaiming and Championing Your Inner Child.* Bantam Books, 1990.

Buetter, Dan. *The Blue Zones Solution: Eating and Living Like the World's Healthiest People.* The National Geographic Society, 2015.

Buzan, Tony and Barry. *The Mind Map Book: How to Use Radiant Thinking to Maximize Your Brain's Untapped Potential.* Dutton, 1994.

Byrne, Lorna, *Angels in My Hair: The True Story of a Modern-Day Irish Mystic.* Random House, 2008, 2011.

Cameron, Julia. *The Artist's Way: A Spiritual Path to Higher Creativity.* Tarcher/Putnam, 1992.

Capacchione, Lucia, Ph.D. *The Power of Your Other Hand: A Course in Channeling the Inner Wisdom of the Right Brain.* Revised Ed. New Page Books, 2001.

Chödrön, Pema. *Fail, Fail Again, Fail Better: Wise Advice for Leaning into the Unknown.* Sounds True, 2015.

Eddy, Mary Baker. *Science and Health with Key to the Scriptures.* 1875. The First Church of Christ, Scientist, 1934.

Fillmore, Charles. *Prosperity.* 1936. Unity Books, 1980.

Fox, Emmet. *Find and Use Your Inner Power.* Harper San Francisco, 1941.

Gawain, Shakti. *Creative Visualization: Use the Power of Your Imagination to Create What You Want in Your Life.* New World Library, 2002.

Godin, Seth. *What to Do When it's Your Turn (and it's Always Your Turn).* Pub. not identified; Vancouver, B.C., 2014.

Hawkins, David R., M.D., Ph.D. *Power vs. Force: the Hidden Determinants of Human Behavior.* Revised Ed., Hay House, Inc. 2002.

Hay, Louise. *Heal Your Body.* Hay House, Inc., 2014.

Hicks, Esther and Jerry. *Ask and it is Given: Learning to Manifest Your Desires.* Hay House, Inc., 2004.

Holmes, Ernest. *The Science of Mind: A Philosophy, A Faith, A Way of Life.* 1938. Tarcher/Putnam, 1966.

Holmes, Tammy J. *Remembering One, Once Again: Twelve Principles That Will Change Your Life.* Tammy J. Holmes, 2012.

Jeffers, Susan, Ph.D., *Feel the Fear and Do It Anyway.* Fawcett Books, 1987.

Kane, Peter. *The Monogamy Challenge: Creating and Keeping Intimacy.* Relationship Transformations Press, 2010.

Katie, Byron and Stephen Mitchell. *Loving What Is: Four Questions That Can Change Your Life.* Three Rivers Press, 2002.

Lerner, Harriet G., Ph.D. *The Dance of Anger: A Woman's Guide to Changing the Patterns of Intimate Relationships.* Harper & Row, 1985.

Linn, Denise. *Sacred Space: Clearing and Enhancing the Energy of your Home.* Ballantine Books, 1995.

McTaggart, Lynne. *The Intention Experiment: Using Your Thoughts to Change Your Life and the World.* Free Press, 2007.

Mercola, Joseph, M.D., *Effortless Healing: 9 Simple Ways to Sidestep Illness, Shed Excess Weight, and Help Your Body Fix Itself.* Harmony Books, 2016.

Murphy, Joseph, Ph.D., D.D. *The Power of Your Sub-Conscious Mind.* Ed. and rev. by Arthur R. Pell, Ph.D. Prentice Hall, 2008.

Newberg, Andrew, M.D., and Mark Robert Waldman. *How Enlightenment Changes Your Brain: The New Science of Transformation.* Random House, 2016.

Osteen, Joel. *I Declare: 31 Promises to Speak Over Your Life.* FaithWords, 2012.

Owen, Amanda. *The Power of Receiving: A Revolutionary Approach to Giving Yourself the Life You Want and Deserve.* Tarcher/Penguin, 2010.

Ray, Sondra. *I Deserve Love: How Affirmations Can Guide You to Personal Fulfillment.* Celestial Arts, 1976.

Roman, Sanaya. *Living with Joy: Keys to Personal Power & Spiritual Transformation.* H. J. Kramer, Inc., 1986.

Sands, Karen, MCC, BCC. *Visionaries Have Wrinkles: Conversations with Wise Women Who Are Reshaping the Future.* Broad Minded Publishing, 2012.

Secunda, Victoria. *When You and Your Mother Can't Be Friends: Resolving the Most Complicated Relationship of Your Life.* Dell Publishing, 1990.

Spalding, Baird T. *Life & Teaching of the Masters of the Far East.* 1927. DeVorss & Co., 1972.

Tibbets, Dick with Steve Halliday, *Forgive to Live: How Forgiveness Can Save Your Life.* Integrity Pub., 2006.

Virtue, Doreen, Ph.D. *Healing with the Angels: How the Angels Can Assist You in Every Area of Your Life.* Hay House, Inc., 1999.

Walsch, Neale Donald. *When Everything Changes, Change Everything: In a Time of Turmoil, a Pathway to Peace.* EmNin Books, 2009.

Williamson, Marianne. *A Return to Love: Reflections on the Principles of A Course In Miracles*. HarperPerennial, 1992.

Zukav, Gary and Linda Francis. *The Heart of the Soul: Emotional Awareness.* Fireside/Simon & Schuster, 2001.

On-line and other resources

Dailyword – a Unity publication

John Bradshaw – http://www.johnbradshaw.com

Christian Science – christianscience.com

Chan, Dharma Drum Mountain – www.dharmadrum.org

Chan, Riverside Chan Meditation Group – riversidechan.org

Dick Sutphen, hypnosis and metaphysics – https://www.dicksutphen.org/

Edgar Cayce – http://www.edgarcayce.org/

Kushi Institute, Macrobiotics – www.kushiinstitute.org

Lisa A. Alzo, writer, lecturer, genealogist – http://www.lisaalzo.com/

Mindmapping – www.tonybuzan.com

Peter Kane, Relationship Transformations – www.rebirthing.com

Peter Yue, Universal Chi Gong – http://www.chigong.com/

Real Colors Website – https://realcolors.org/

Science of Mind Magazine: Guide for Spiritual Living – scienceofmind.com

Silva Method – https://www.silvamethod.com

Unity – www.unity.org

Veola Vazquez, psychologist, author, inspirational speaker – www.veolavazquez.com

Voice Dialog International, Hal and Sidra Stone – http://www.voicedialogueinternational.com/

About the Author

Sheryl A. Stradling is a pioneer in the holistic health movement. She has lived and championed a holistic lifestyle throughout her adult life. She is a Reiki, breathwork and Chi Gong practitioner, organic gardener and certified herbalist. She has facilitated women's spiritual and personal-growth groups, taught natural foods nutrition and cooking, and assisted individuals in healing themselves physically, emotionally and spiritually.

Sheryl's spiritual journey began at thirteen when she dedicated her life to God. Although she didn't comprehend the magnitude of her commitment, she recognized that she was embarking on a transformational journey. She taught herself to meditate and use self-hypnosis to gain greater control over her emotions. She has continued her spiritual path to inner awareness and healing through daily practice.

Always naturally curious, Sheryl has grown and evolved through a variety of disciplines: practical, rational and intuitive training; marriage and divorce; single-parenting; various therapies; and personal and experiential growth training.

Sheryl has written journals since she was twelve. She continues to use them as a means to express and work through emotions, create and use positive affirmations, understand dreams, and to invoke the power of the subconscious to realize greater spiritual truth. Through her writing, she accesses her inner wisdom, that of *SpiritWoman*, and follows her spiritual guidance to achieve greater self-understanding and help others.

Sheryl's background includes a family of educators, writers, artists and musicians. She grew up in the Pacific Northwest, and is descended from Washington State pioneers. Her family has called the metro Seattle area home for over 100 years.

A perennial student, Sheryl enjoys reading, and studying metaphysics, genealogy and herbal lore. She relishes being outdoors in nature where she enjoys jogging, studying plants and working in her experimental garden. She is also an abstract artist, and derives her inspiration from the natural world.

Education: M.A. in Humanities

For more information, please see Sheryl's website:

www.sherylstradling.com